AF316774

HEALING SYMPHONY

MY DISCOVERY OF HEALING
IN THE SILENCE OF MUSIC

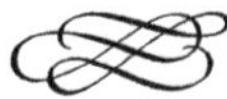

DIDIER FRANÇOIS

YUNUS PUBLISHING

CONTENTS

PROLOGUE

Imagine the gift of a magical solution to life's challenges, or immersing yourself in an enchanting world of live music where a story of healing and transformation unfolds. Is there a mysterious force beyond our sensory limits that resonates in the realm of music? Perhaps this force moves like an invisible wave through our emotions, sometimes evoking joy or sorrow, while at other times bringing peace that allows us to sway to the rhythm of silences, as if the world around us suddenly freezes in time. It is often observed that the impact of music is underestimated, despite this art form's ability to penetrate and influence the deepest layers of our being.

In various art forms, from cinema to theater, music serves as a guiding force that goes beyond mere background noise. Its ability to define a scene, accentuate emotions, or tell a story transcends what we can rationalize. It is not just an accompaniment but an integral part of the overall experience. Millions are invested in finding the perfect musical accompaniment to influence our purchasing behavior, which is powerful evidence of the profound impact sound has on our mood and decision-making.

Ironically, the idea of external forces in music is often dismissed as airy or elusive, confined to what we can understand rationally. As an artist with both artistic impulses and a deep analytical curiosity, I have dedicated my life to understanding the magic of creation. Over the years, I have sought answers, and science has provided me with countless insights that I am eager to share with you in the pages of this book.

The universal language of music can reveal more secrets than we can imagine. I propose that we delve deeper together into the mystical power of music and discover the hidden dimensions that lead us to a deeper understanding of the world around us. Melodies and rhythms not only bring joy but also open the doors to a universe of wisdom that can only be revealed through the enchantment of music. Let us embark together on this harmonious journey of discovery.

Have you ever rediscovered the essence of life, confronted with the question: what are the true necessities? Are basic needs like food, drink, and sleep really the only driving forces that keep us alive? Or is there a deeper meaning woven into the fabric of existence, something not only perceptible by our senses but also transcending their limitations?

In the enchanting world of live music, a story of healing and transformation emerges, where the power of sounds and tones embraces and nourishes the soul. This book is a journey through the healing dimensions of music, an exploration of harmonies capable of easing the burdens of daily life and opening the path to well-being.

In the midst of this musical odyssey, it is crucial to recognize that the solutions presented here, however simple they may be, are not always easy. In our quest for healing, the simplest answers are often the most effective, but not necessarily the easiest to embrace. As we experience the enchantment of sound, let us remember that the simplicity of this healing journey does not mean it is without effort. It requires dedication, self-reflection, and a willingness to explore the deeper layers of ourselves. Music does not offer an escape but rather serves as a guide on our journey toward inner healing.

This journey involves a deep analysis of the challenges encountered in our pursuit of well-being, where the simplicity of the proposed solutions should not be underestimated. It takes courage to confront the heart of our challenges and to embrace the healing power of live music as a powerful companion on this path.

This book is not a promise of a magical solution to all of life's challenges. It is an invitation to embrace the power of live music as a healing instrument, a winding path toward well-being. Together, let us discover how simple and timeless harmonies not only enchant the ears but also soothe the soul.

Not being a scientist, my approach to the magic of music is infused with my own experiences and personal beliefs. I draw inspiration from scientific insights and translate them into my own understanding of the musical world.

This is a personal quest, where some ideas may seem complex while others are seen as simple and accessible. I would be delighted to share my experiences and personal beliefs with you and explore the rich world of music. Allow yourself to be immersed in the captivating power of sound as we uncover the deeper meanings and hidden possibilities within music. We can experience the magic of music in our lives.

CHAPTER 1

A HARMONIOUS JOURNEY THROUGH LIFE

At the heart of my story lies a journey woven with threads of melody and rhythm, an odyssey of a musician navigating through the diverse landscapes of human experience. My narrative, intertwined with the universal language of music, bears witness to the profound impact of sound on the human soul.

PRELUDE: ORIGIN AND DISCOVERY

As a budding musician, my journey began with the discovery of an enchanting world of notes and chords. The first hesitant strokes on the strings or the cautious pressure on the piano keys marked the beginning of a lifelong friendship with music. Those early days were filled with the innocent curiosity of a beginner, exploring the vast terrain of musical possibilities.

ACT 1: MOMENTS OF JOY AND HARMONY

In the symphony of life, music became a constant ally during moments of unbridled joy: celebrating personal victories or savoring the collective triumphs of life, melodies resonated with the essence of pleasure. From the lively tempo of exuberance to the soothing lullabies of my mind, music became the soundtrack of moments worth cherishing.

ACT 2: ECHOES OF SORROW AND HEALING

Life's journey is not just a crescendo of joy; it also includes the delicate tones of sadness and melancholy. In times of sorrow, music became a comfort, a refuge where emotions could be expressed without judgment. Each melancholic note resonated in the depths of my soul, offering a catharsis that pointed the way to healing.

INTERMEZZO: CONTEMPLATION AND GROWTH

As this musical journey progressed, moments of contemplation became interludes between the movements of life. Through the subtleties of composition, the power of reflection and self-discovery revealed itself within me. Music, in its diverse patterns, mirrored the complexity of my thoughts and pushed me to embrace the nuances of my own evolution.

MY STORY: A MELODIOUS TAPESTRY

The chapters of my story are intricately woven into the fabric of musical notes. Each composition tells a tale of resilience, growth, and an unwavering quest for artistic expression. The melodies, reflecting personal triumphs and trials, form a symphony that continues to evolve day by day.

THE PRESENT: HARMONY WITH THE MOMENT

In the rhythm of life, the present has emerged as the focal point of my musical journey. The realization that trues connection with the essence of music occurs in the present moment has been profound. By fully immersing myself in the present, I discovered that music acts as a bridge between the inner self and the outer world.

Embracing the present through music is like tuning in to the frequency of life itself. A harmonious coexistence with the surrounding vibrations emerges, creating a tapestry of sounds that encapsulates the beauty of existence. In this harmonious fusion, I found a haven of mindfulness, where the past and the future fade away, leaving only the resonant echoes of the current musical note.

CODA: AN UNFOLDING MUSICAL ODYSSEY

My story connects with the present as the melody of life continues. The chapters remain open, waiting to be filled with new compositions and experiences. Amid the twists and turns of existence, the musician within me traverses the path of an eternal symphony. I seek harmony in every note and find comfort there.

My musical journey began at the age of four when I expressed to my parents my desire to play the violin. To them, it seemed like an impossible mission at that age, but within me was an unwavering determination. In a time of indulged children, I followed my own path. Against all odds, I chose the violin, despite being enrolled in a preschool rhythm class where I was supposed to thrive creatively. The sound of exploratory noises was like a short circuit, fueled by my inflexible will. A miracle occurred when I told Santa Claus that I still wanted to play the violin. My determination was rewarded, and a drawing of a beautiful violin adorned my letter to Santa. This was my first creative triumph, proof that firmness and self-belief could work wonders.

Although my parents were not musicians, they sparked my interest by taking me to concerts by a symphony orchestra and a jazz club. A cardboard box was given to me as a drum set to accompany the jazz drummer, marking my first musical experience. During this period at Yale University, where my father conducted research and my mother filled her studio with batiks and oil paintings, the seed for the symbiosis of art and research was planted. Was it my stubbornness, or was I driven by a mysterious childlike force? During those years, I saw myself as the Zorro of music, determined to save the world with my magical powers. The innovative 1970s laid the foundation for my eccentric existence, where art and music became a calling reflecting my most intrinsic purpose.

As I grew older, I began to reflect on the winding paths of my childhood as an imposed calling. I often wondered why I was different, why I clashed with imposed authorities. Through my struggle against rules and limitations, I was unconsciously seeking my own freedom, a fundamental element for my future salvation. Today, I understand that this childhood, steeped in eccentric determination, was not merely defiance but a pursuit of deeper truths. My struggle against societal frameworks and my search for truth were attempts to comprehend the deeper objectives of my musical quest.

CHAPTER 2

THE INTRIGUING REALM OF A
REVOLUTIONARY VIOLIN TECHNIQUE

My most epic challenge unfolded when I began to realize that my instrument could not simply be tamed. The traditional path, often rigid, starting at music school and continuing through the conservatory, emphasized absolute mastery of one's instrument. For hours, I tried to capture the sound, the notes that danced like musical dreams in my mind, and the perfect bowing that sliced through the notes like a work of art.

However, it seemed that my own will thwarted me again and again. With each attempt, I found myself disappointed, brought down, like a fearless cowboy determined to ride an untamed mustang, repeatedly kissing the ground while the spirited horse galloped away, almost laughing at the human attempts at control. The violin, as a vibrant entity, eluded my grasp, and I came to the conclusion that no instrument can be fully tamed.

It's futile to try to control my violin; I must guide it. It's more like a winding dance, a symbiosis between the human and the instrument, where I lead my musical companion in the direction I envision. A metaphor comes to mind: skating on a graceful pond, giving a powerful push and then gliding effortlessly on the ice.

The blades under my shoes, sharp and well-honed, trace a path effortlessly on the ice, and I can't help but think of Newton's first law: an object in motion wants to stay in motion. This realization not only transformed my artistic journey but also opened the door to a surprising world of freedom and musical expression that I had never envisioned before.

I dive into into the enchanting realm of instrumental truth, where my relationship with the violin goes beyond mere musical interaction. It's a poetic dance between human and instrument, a fusion of soul and sound that reaches toward the essence of musical expression.

Sometimes, like a sparkling paradox, I whisper to my students: "You are not a violin, but a human being." A seemingly simple remark that touches the heart of the unique partnership we share. For, imagine if a violin could speak; wouldn't it say, "I understand better than you how this should sound"?

Take a moment to reflect on the fascinating journey of vibrations, a story that begins at the string, travels through the bridge, and seamlessly merges into the soundboard. There, it forms a perfect symbiosis with the surrounding air, a magical marriage of tones and resonance. Like a flock of starlings dancing gracefully around a steeple, the sounds then take flight through the f-holes and become one with the air again. They find their harmony in the acoustics of the space where we tell our musical story.

This deep knowledge, transcending the mere understanding of the violin, lies far beyond my reach. Here, the luthier's craftsmanship comes into play, an experienced guide who brings the instrument to life with an intrinsic understanding of sound and resonance. The violin is born into a world where my hands are essential for interpreting the music that awakens in my soul each morning, yearning to be expressed.

In these moments of fusion, effortless agility emerges, a play of identities where I am myself, and my violin is what it is. This partnership transcends the conventional relationship between the player and the instrument; it's a symbiotic pact in which I offer my skills, and my violin shares its profound knowledge. Here, in this unique understanding, true musical magic comes to life—an enchanting interplay between human and instrument that goes beyond the limits of mere technique.

When I try to fight against the natural flow of movement and forcefully control the violin, I become frustrated because the instrument doesn't respond to my wishes. I am also confronted with a fundamental principle that could have led to satisfying results had I better understood and applied its internal workings. This unsuccessful attempt results in a tense mental strain on the strings, a phenomenon that also occurs with other instruments, like the air in a wind instrument, the skin of a drum, or even the air passing through vocal cords while singing.

However, this tense attitude is contrary to the natural movement inherent in all matter. Just as electrons effortlessly orbit around the nucleus of an atom for infinite durations, a string vibrates just as easily when allowed to move freely. Under pressure, however, this natural movement is hindered. The same applies to other musical instruments, where air must flow freely to produce a beautiful and harmonious sound.

My first mastery and application of this technique during a concert was an unforgettable experience. It was a magnificent solo concert in a castle in Schoten, Belgium. The hall was filled with an attentive audience, the walls radiating history and elegance, and there was an atmosphere of complete silence in the air. I felt a slight tension in my chest, but also a deep calm, a confidence born from years of practice.

The path to this moment had been long and difficult. As Lao Tzu says in the Tao Te Ching, a book about wisdom and balance, the path to mastery is paved with ten thousand actions. Every note I played, every repetition, every mistake, and every correction was a step on this path. It had taken years of patience and perseverance to perfect the technique, to truly allow the sound of my violin to resonate with the souls of the listeners.

I opened the concert with the sound of a simple, very old wooden metronome. As the pleasant and calm tempo set in, I saw smiles appear on some faces in the audience. The ticking brought a serene atmosphere to the hall, a perfect prelude to what was to follow. Then, I took my mobile phone, which I always have on stage, tuned my instrument, and placed it under one of the metronome's legs. As a result, the metronome no longer maintained its regular rhythm. The once beautifully binary and regular ticking suddenly became asymmetrical as the unbalanced base disrupted the movement of the metronome's arm. This created a new, unpredictable rhythm. This change in the ticking introduced an element of surprise and transformed the static repetition into a living, organic pulse played by my clear partner.

I used this new, unpredictable rhythm to perform my first original composition of the evening: "Impermanenza" or "Transience," a piece that embodies the concept of impermanence—the understanding that everything in life is fleeting and temporary. It refers to the inevitable finitude and decay of things, people, and events. This idea is often linked to the transience of human life, nature, and material possessions, evoking a philosophical and existential reflection on the nature of existence and the temporality of everything around us.

The ice was broken, and I felt the audience being drawn into the music with intense focus. The unusual introduction had added an unexpected depth, a sense of transience and change that perfectly aligned with the title of my composition. The room was filled with a soft glow as I took up my violin. The instrument felt both familiar and new in my hands, as if it were about to reveal a secret that had remained hidden until that moment. I took a deep breath, inhaling the scent of old wood and resin, and placed the bow on the string.

With a light, fluid motion, I drew the bow across the string. A warm, rich sound filled the room, expanding and multiplying with a complexity that momentarily surprised me. The harmonics seemed to dance in layers over one another, like waves in an invisible sea, each with its own story and color. The violin was no longer just producing sound; it was creating a vibrant palette of emotions and images.

This time was different. Every note I played carried a depth I had never felt before. The sound had taken on a new dimension, a richness that touched the soul and resonated in every fiber of my being. It wasn't just music; it was a dialogue between the violin and my inner world, a wordless conversation that went straight to the heart.

As the note lingered, I noticed how the resonance spread. The sound weaved its way through the air and nestled into the hearts of the listeners. There was a subtle vibration, an almost imperceptible tremor that persisted long after the note had faded. The sound didn't seem to end with the note but lingered, an ethereal echo that continued in the listener's consciousness.

The silence after the note was as powerful as the note itself. It was a charged silence, full of unspoken emotions and thoughts, as if the sound was still present in the space between the sound waves. I observed the audience around me, their eyes closed, surrendering to the aftereffects of the music. It was clear that the violin's resonance had touched their souls, a healing symphony that created a deep connection between me, my instrument, and them.

In that moment, I realized the true power of music. It wasn't just about technique or perfection, but about letting go and surrendering. By gently sliding the bow across the string, I gave the music the space to breathe, to find its own path, and to reveal an unprecedented richness. It was a collaboration between the instrument and me, a symbiosis that unveiled something deeper.

As the final echoes of the music faded away, I felt a deep sense of satisfaction. The sound of my violin had not only filled the space but also the souls of those who listened. It was a reminder of the power of sound, a symphony that continued to resonate in the hearts of all who experienced it. In this resonance, I found a new source of inspiration, a continuous quest for the healing power of music.

Have you ever imagined, or perhaps even experienced, the sensation of drinking a century-old wine, crafted from ancient vines with love and respect for nature? Imagine delicately holding the glass in your hand, swirling its contents. You bring the glass to your nose and breathe deeply, the aromas of dried fruits, earthy notes, and subtle spices enchanting your senses. Then, with eager anticipation, you bring the glass to your lips and let the first sip of this precious liquid touch your palate. A symphony of flavors dances on your tongue, each sip revealing new nuances and the depth of the cellar.

But it's not just the taste that impresses. It's the experience itself, the moment when the world stops as you focus on every sensory perception. It's the aftertaste that lingers, for days, maybe even years, etched into your memory like a precious jewel of pleasure.

With just one sip of this refined wine, your imagination seems to take flight. Suddenly, you find yourself among the vines, feeling the warm sun on your face and inhaling the scents of the terroir floating in the air. You even hear the crunch of gravel underfoot as you walk through the vineyard, your thoughts drifting toward the intense beauty of nature.

But then, like a twist in a captivating story, you are suddenly surprised by the coolness of the "chai," the wine cellar. As you pass through the door, the scent of the cellar envelops your senses. It's a blend of damp earth, wood, and the promise of hidden treasures waiting patiently to be discovered. Your eyes adjust to the dim light filtering through the cellar as you immerse yourself in the mysterious atmosphere filling the space.

A single sip of wine can remarkably stimulate your imagination and awaken a delightful sensory experience. It evokes a profound sense of wonder about the power of our minds and how our senses can take us on a journey to distant lands, even when we remain physically in one place.

Just as wine takes you on a journey through vineyards and cellars, music can transport you in a similar way. With each note, each chord, you are plunged into a world of emotions and imagination. You traverse a soundscape where each melody reveals a new adventure, and each harmony unveils a deeper layer of the story.

Much like the vineyards that grow patiently and mature before yielding their precious fruits, music requires time and devotion to fully bloom. It's a process of growth and development, where every note, every melody contributes to the richness of the symphony. Just as fine wine improves with age, music reveals increasingly deep layers and rich flavors with each new listening experience.

It was a moment of intense emotion when my violin teacher, Myriam Quersin, assistant to Arthur Grumiaux at the Conservatory of Brussels, announced that I had the opportunity to play the legendary "Wendling" Stradivarius. It was a tribute to my dedication to the violin, a reward for the countless hours of practice and discipline I had invested in my music. But when I first touched the strings of this famous violin, I was faced with a disappointment I had not anticipated.

In my hands, the "Wendling" Stradivarius felt strange and unfamiliar. The instrument seemed to have its own voice, a voice I could not immediately find. My fingers hesitated as I tried to play, but the sounds that emerged were not the warm, rich tones I had expected. My playing sounded stiff and forced, far from the fluidity and resonance I was used to with my own violin.

The challenge I encountered playing on my teacher's "Strad" was unlike anything I had experienced before. It was a profound sense of disappointment when I realized that I played better on my own violin than on this famous Stradivarius. It seemed that my own technique was holding me back, as if I were trapped by the rigid rules and technical demands needed to do justice to this legendary violin.

The room where we played, with the Steinway piano beside me, exuded a 1960s modernity, with low-slung furniture and a beautiful view of its garden of pink flowers. My violin teacher, a woman of unmatched knowledge and patience, watched with a mix of understanding and encouragement as I struggled with my own limitations and expectations.

I felt like I had gold in my hands but lead in my heart. The myth of the Stradivarius seemed too great, my expectations too high. But when I finally surrendered to the instrument, something magical happened. Under the guidance of my teacher, I slowly began to understand and respect the "Wendling" Stradivarius. And then it happened: a spark of understanding, a moment of successful connection between me and the violin.

Heaven opened up to me, an unforgettable moment of pure ecstasy. Then, I had the chance to play on this violin for months, and each time was a dual experience. This perfect instrument required perfect technique to come alive, but once I reached that level, the harmonics became remarkably rich, and the sound continued to resonate in my ears and memories for a long time.

I realized that my approach needed to change. Instead of trying to control the violin, I had to guide it. It was a dance of giving and taking, a symbiosis between the human and the instrument where I had to let go of my technical skills and allow the violin the space to express itself as it wished. It was a new chapter in my musical journey, a chapter that taught me that true art is not just about perfection, but also about finding a deeper connection with the instrument and the music it produces.

Playing the "Wendling" Stradivarius, I delved deeper into the boundless beauty of this extraordinary instrument. But my discoveries went beyond the simple sound of the violin. They reached the depths of my soul and creativity, bringing a new source of inspiration and joy into my life. This experience marked the beginning of a continuous quest for the true meaning of music and art, a quest I pursued alongside the renowned Joseph Nagyváry.

Joseph Nagyváry is a legend in the field of violin research. His obsession with the sound of Stradivarius violins is almost mythical, and his laboratory in Texas is a sanctuary for luthiers and musicians from around the world. When I first contacted him, I felt as though I had opened a door to a hidden world, a world where the secrets of the old masters and the mysteries of violin sound were revealed.

One of the most fascinating aspects of my research, alongside Nagyváry, was experimenting with the influence of a "loose" bow stroke on the sound of the violin. I proposed adding this aspect to the research, believing that the way the bow moved across the strings had a profound effect on the instrument's resonance and harmony. Nagyváry was immediately intrigued by my proposal, and together we embarked on a series of experiments to test the theory.

For many hours, we worked together in his laboratory, analyzing the sound of different violins and experimenting with various playing techniques. It was an intense period of discovery and growth, during which I not only deepened my understanding of the "loose" sound of the violin but also improved my own skills as a musician.

Ultimately, we arrived at an astonishing conclusion: a loose bow stroke indeed had a significant influence on the sound of the violin. This revelation changed my entire approach to violin practice and gave me new perspectives on the subtleties of timbre and resonance.

In the spirit of discovery and innovation, I expanded my collaboration with Alex Piltz, a renowned luthier specializing in the study of ancient instruments, using modern technologies. Piltz and I worked together on developing the nyckelharpa, using his expertise in analyzing historical instruments and my musical experience. Together, we refined the sound of my instrument and took it to a new level by applying innovative techniques and thorough research. This collaboration not only enriched my own playing technique but also contributed to the evolution of my keyed violin, the nyckelharpa, as an instrument, allowing us to further explore the limits of its sonic capabilities.

But the most important aspect was not only the scientific discovery itself but also the personal growth I experienced during this process. I learned to listen to music with an open mind and a curious heart, and to appreciate the beauty of sound in all its forms and variations.

This moment marked a turning point in my career. Previously, I was often labeled a "dreamer" because of my focus on the subtle aspects of timbre and resonance that were not easily quantifiable. However, with the scientific proof of the influence of a loose bow stroke on the sound of the violin, my approach was no longer dismissed as esoteric or subjective. It was a satisfying confirmation of what I had always felt: even the smallest details of performance and technique can have a significant impact on the sound and expression of an instrument.

In the years that followed, I continued to refine my approach to violin practice, fueled by the insights I gained in Nagyváry and Piltz's laboratories. As I advanced in my musical journey, I remained acutely aware of the profound connection between science and art, and the endless possibilities of music to touch our hearts and souls.

My idea of letting the sound of the violin flow and guiding the instrument rather than attempting to control it aligns closely with Lao Zi's (also known as Lao Tzu) philosophy of Wu Wei. Lao Zi is a legendary Chinese philosopher regarded as the founder of Taoism. He is believed to have lived in the 6th century BCE, although some sources suggest he might have been a contemporary of Confucius or lived even later. His most famous work is the *Tao Te Ching* (also spelled *Dao De Jing*), a classic text containing profound wisdom about life, governance, and the nature of the universe.

One of the key concepts in the *Tao Te Ching* is Wu Wei, which can be translated as "non-action" or "action without effort." Wu Wei does not literally mean doing nothing but rather acting in harmony with the natural flow of life without forced effort or constraint. It is a way of being that aligns with the Tao, the eternal and ineffable order of the universe.

Wu Wei encourages us not to force or push. Instead of clinging desperately to a specific outcome, we learn to trust the natural course of events. It is about finding balance and respecting the natural rhythms and cycles of life. Wu Wei also means being flexible and open to change. You act spontaneously and respond to what is necessary in the moment rather than sticking to rigid plans and expectations. By acting according to Wu Wei, you often achieve more with less effort. Just as water finds its way through obstacles by following the path of least resistance, we can also reach our goals more effectively by moving with the natural flow.

Wu Wei promotes a state of inner peace and harmony. By

accepting what is and moving with the natural rhythms, we experience less stress and more satisfaction. Wu Wei can be applied to various aspects of life, from work and relationships to personal growth and creativity. At work, it means learning to prioritize tasks, delegate, and trust the process, which often leads to better results and a more relaxed work environment. In personal relationships, Wu Wei encourages us not trying to change others or force situations, but to communicate openly and respectfully and let relationships develop organically. Personal development according to Wu Wei means giving yourself space to grow and learn without pushing too hard. You trust your inner wisdom and intuition to find your way. As mentioned previously in the context of music, Wu Wei in creativity means allowing yourself to flow with your creative process without being constrained by excessive control or perfectionism.

This philosophy of Wu Wei is not limited to playing the violin but extends to all aspects of our lives. How often have we tried to shape circumstances to our will, struggling against the flow of life instead of adapting to it? We might find ourselves stuck in a job that doesn't fulfill us, yet we cling to it out of fear of the unknown. Or we might try to force a relationship that isn't good for us simply because we are reluctant to let go.

Have you ever been stuck in traffic? Instead of getting frustrated and trying to control the situation by honking and shouting, you can choose to go with the flow of the traffic and patiently wait for the situation to improve. At that moment, you are experiencing Wu Wei—letting go of the desire to control and accepting the natural course of events.

Applying this philosophy teaches us to trust the inherent wisdom of the universe and to act in harmony with the natural flow of life. It is an ongoing journey of self-discovery and growth, where we gradually learn to let go and follow the dance of life. Just as we find deeper satisfaction and joy in our lives when we embrace Wu Wei, playing the violin also reveals deeper meaning and beauty when we relinquish control. I discovered that I needed to change my approach to the violin to bring out the true beauty of the "Wendling" Stradivarius. Instead of trying to strictly control every note and movement, I learned that I needed to guide the violin and give it the space to express itself.

The process of becoming an expert in movement indeed required a significant investment of time and energy. It was not simply about repeating without purpose or direction. Rather, it was a conscious journey of self-discovery and growth, where each hour of practice offered an opportunity to delve deeper into the subtle nuances of movement. By surrendering to this process, I began to realize that letting go did not mean doing nothing. Instead, it was an active choice to release control and trust the inherent wisdom of the movement itself. It was a transition from tense effort to effortless surrender, allowing me to be guided by the natural flow of my own inner rhythm.

This approach not only transformed my playing but also led to personal growth. By learning to listen to the subtle nuances of sound and resonance, I developed a deeper appreciation for the beauty of music in all its forms and variations. I learned to listen to music with an open mind and a curious heart and to appreciate the aesthetics of sound without forcing it. This principle of letting go applies not only to technical skill but also to emotional expression. Music is a language of emotions, and by surrendering to the feelings we wish to convey, rather than trying to control them, we can create a deeper connection with our audience. We become not only performers but also mediators of emotion and meaning.

Furthermore, Wu Wei helps us accept mistakes and imperfections as a natural part of the learning process and life itself. Instead of focusing on what went wrong, we can shift our attention to the joy of playing and expressing our creativity. This fosters not only a healthier approach to practice and performance but also contributes to our personal growth and satisfaction as musicians. In summary, by applying the philosophy of Wu Wei to music, we learn to let go of control and be guided by the natural flow of music. This leads to a richer and more meaningful musical experience, both for the performer and the audience. It is an invitation to connect more deeply with ourselves, with music, and with the universe, and to embrace the beauty of effortless action.

The natural sound, once freed and shaped by a multitude of audible and inaudible tones, emerges when the sound is free to resonate. A free and unobstructed flow of sound is comparable to a clear phone line, whereas a poor connection hinders understanding at the other end. In the world of music, sound is not just an artistic medium but also a powerful means of communication. However, the smooth communication of sounds is disrupted when tensions arise in the field.

In my quest to understand the delicate balance between control and freedom on the violin, I often reflect on a remarkable historical fact that highlighted these principles in an unexpected way. During World War II, a period of intense tension and conflict, an incident occurred involving the radio frequencies of the German armed forces.

Above the front lines, the German and Allied forces relied on radio communication to coordinate their strategies, plan missions, and exchange information. Both British and German pilots realized this was a vulnerability, and they devised plans to disrupt the enemy's radio frequencies, hoping to hinder communication and reduce the effectiveness of bombing raids.

Both sides faced interference on their radio frequencies, leading to confusion, misunderstandings, and failed missions. They had to battle an invisible enemy that not only limited their physical movements but also undermined their communication capabilities.

The British pilots then adopted a new strategy. Instead of desperately trying to control the disrupted frequencies, they chose a freer and more creative approach. They developed special codes, used different frequencies, and made constant adjustments to bypass the German interference. This improvisation and the ability to adapt in the heat of battle gave the British pilots an advantage and restored their ability to communicate effectively.

This historical example reflects the paradox of control and freedom. Sometimes, when we cling tightly to control, we encounter unexpected obstacles that hinder our progress. The ability to let go, to improvise creatively, and to adapt to changing circumstances, as the English pilots did, can lead to unexpected triumphs and a deeper understanding of the delicate balance between control and freedom. This valuable lesson also applies to my musical journey, where letting go of strict control of the violin sometimes opens new paths for expression and artistic freedom.

The freedom I grant myself by relinquishing control opens the door to another dimension, a dimension that I do not fully master but that adds profound meaning to my music. It is a journey into the unknown, where sounds flow freely, communicate, and resonate with a deeper significance that transcends my quest for control.

Rooted in my musical odyssey, a distinct principle manifests, surpassing the confines of notes on paper and unfolding like a choreography of collaboration. It is a symphony of body parts—arms, wrists, hands, fingers, upper body—a harmonious play resulting from the fluid movement of the bow. Like a conductor, I must coordinate each "instrument" of my body, guiding the melodies of sound, rhythm, and emotion.

Analogous to dissecting a dance movement, where each muscle is dedicated to guiding you step by step to your destination, I approach my musical creation similarly. My goal is clear in my mind: the desired sound, the notes resonating with my vision, the articulation reflecting my musical language, and the structure of phrases shaping the direction, akin to spoken language. In this symphony of expression, each note can come to life effortlessly, merely by loosening the reins of strict control.

Just like a journey to a destination, where you need to focus on arriving, the process of musical creation requires a similar approach. However, clinging to rigid control results in a polished but monotonous interpretation. It resembles a stiff and repetitive note, lacking the sparkle in the eyes, the spirit, or the magic of the piece. Under the constraint of control, music suffers from stiffness, sounding unfortunate and cerebral.

On the other hand, embracing freedom reveals something always present, waiting to blossom: discovering a hidden layer concealing a precious thing—my intrinsic ability as a musician to inspire others. It's about mastering my music effortlessly, not through strict control, but by embracing freedom and uncovering what has always been there, waiting to be fully revealed.

In the deep vaults of my musical quest, a captivating spectacle unfolds where the will to succeed, a mental force of epic proportions, dances with the subconscious, like two invisible partners in an enchanting waltz. The performance takes place on a vast stage formed by the iceberg-shaped landscape of my cognitive brain, with only the tip visible above the water's surface while the immense mass lies hidden in the unfathomable depths of my instinctive nature. In my quest for control over every subtle musical detail, unexpected obstacles sometimes arise, obscuring the view of the much greater force—a force operating at the speed of thought, with the precision of a clock and the infallibility of a compass.

Forging this inner strength is not a random event but rather an art that I refine through relentless repetition. It is a cyclical symphony that began on that very first day when my fingers delicately touched the strings. Like an Olympic pool being patiently filled, drop by drop, my subconscious is saturated with the knowledge of each note, each bow stroke, each musical nuance. It is a gradual process where my inner pool becomes eventually saturated and gains autonomy to act independently, like an experienced swimmer navigating effortlessly through the undulating sea of musicality.

The Olympic pool analogy transcends mere rhetoric and embodies the time-consuming nature of this process, especially for aspiring young violinists. Filling this pool with knowledge requires not only time and devotion. The shining good news at the end of this musical tunnel: once knowledge is ingrained in the fingers, it becomes an inexhaustible and permanent source. Like cultivating a lush garden of musical wisdom, where the flowers thrive under the subtle movement of my bow and each vibration of the strings, a garden that not only colors my musical journey but also enchants those who enter it.

In this approach unfolds a sequence of discovery. This technique, seemingly simple, unlocks like a mysterious key to mastery. It's embarking on an intriguing journey where, through playing, I reflect the harmony of my daily movements, like a fluid choreography. Each step, each action—opening a door, brushing teeth, handling a knife and fork during a meal— these actions form a familiar symphony that I conduct as a master. Just like the notes of my daily score, played without hesitation and imbued with natural grace.

Reflecting on my childhood brings a smile of recognition. I took adventurous steps, filled with trial and error. Learning these movements required patience and practice, and Every time I fell a valuable lesson on my path to mastery. The memory of those first steps now resonates in the learning of musical first steps, a journey of discovery where each fall becomes a lesson and each rise a triumph of skill learned. Just as learning to walk, playing music is an art that cannot be easily forgotten, except in the case of an unfortunate physical injury that would impede my ability to play.

In my quest for musical mastery, I use these daily movements as a guide. It's like applying a copy-paste method to my neural pathways, a digital replication of the dance between my neurons. This results in the creation of new synaptic connections, a vibrant network of cognitive highways that refine and accelerate my learning ability. The journey reveals a fascinating symbiosis where daily routines harmoniously merge with the art of musical expression, and the ordinary transforms into something extraordinary.

This fascinating technique ultimately aims to let the uncontrollable do its work, a dance of forces that animates the universe and keeps the world in harmony. I become a particle in this cosmic spectacle, a vibrant component that simply needs to move with the larger forces already at work around me. Think of the migration of birds meticulously following the laws of the universe, the flow of water finding its own path, the blooming of flowers with the arrival of spring, and the rest of nature in autumn. In all this, I recognize my role as part of a greater whole, a consciousness that drives me to relinquish the urge to control.

My conviction to play music is deeply rooted and seems pre-programmed in my being. How else could I, as a child, have so determinedly persuaded my parents to allow me to play the violin? It was an inner call, an innate knowledge of becoming the interpreter of a universal language. This language is imbued with emotions conveyed through my playing, an enchanting melody inviting both conscious and unconscious listeners to ride the waves of feeling. Behind the delicate strings lies a key, an entryway to unexplored dimensions waiting to be revealed and explored, like pages of a mysterious book of which I am the storyteller.

CHAPTER 3

MUSIC AS A GATEWAY TO INNER PEACE

*C*an you recall a time when you and your partner stood outside a concert venue, hearts overflowing with anticipation? You had been looking forward to this evening for weeks, ever since you got tickets to a performance that promised to be unforgettable.

Once through the venue's doors, you were captivated by the electric atmosphere, the stage set, and the audience buzzing with excitement, already transported to another world through the magic of music.

Settling into your seats, the anticipation grew with each passing moment. Around you, other spectators exchanged smiles and nods, united in their shared love for music and their anticipation for the upcoming show.

As the lights dimmed, the first notes filled the air, and silence fell over the audience. Whether it was the soothing melodies of a jazz ensemble, the pulsating rhythms of a pop concert, the moving voices of an opera, or the grandeur of a symphony orchestra under the baton of a conductor, you were drawn into the music, completely captivated by the sounds enveloping you.

Over the next hour, you were transported on a journey of emotion and imagination, as the music embraced you. In those moments, you forgot the stresses and worries of daily life, lost in the beauty and power of the present music.

During the intermission, you joined the lively crowd in the lobby, enjoying drinks and snacks while sharing animated discussions about the performance so far. The air was charged with anticipation, the energy of the music still pulsing through your veins.

Returning to your seats for the second half of the concert, you felt a sense of renewal and rejuvenation wash over you. The music touched something deep within you, filling you with a sense of joy and possibility.

And as the final notes resonated through the venue, you stood up, joining the audience in a thunderous ovation. In that moment, you knew you would carry the memory of this magical evening with you forever, a testament to the transformative power of music and the shared experience of a live performance.

Have you ever thought about that euphoria after a concert? I often reflect on this, considering my musical niche—a slow blend of baroque and jazz. No explosive pop rhythms, no ecstasy on the dance floor, no collective singing. Yet, the audience invariably leaves the hall with radiant smiles, exchanging stories about the enchanted experience. It's akin to returning from a vacation, still delighted by the sunny weather, delicious food, and cultural discovery. A respite from the harsh reality of life, perhaps. But is reintegrating into reality an escape, or are we constantly fleeing what we truly need: relaxation, joy and happiness? And what if music, in a unique way, offers dus the chance to come home after a prolonged quest for truth with our eyes closed?

A metamorphosis is underway—a transformation from a dark and gray mood into a vibrant and fulfilled soul. The audience, seemingly seeking to save their lives drowned in fear and worries, leaves the concert hall with renewed resilience. The shared experience, like a waking dream of vacation, lingers in conversations. It's a communal escape to an alternative reality, a respite from daily routines. The audience may have had to navigate through a maze of daily hassles to reach the concert: heavy rain, no parking near the venue, a slightly late babysitter. They had to rush into the hall. Among these challenges lies an opportunity to emotionally engage the audience in the concert's narrative. It's a chance for metamorphosis, an encouragement to recharge and face life with a fresh perspective.

Instead of collapsing into bed exhausted, one falls asleep brimming with zeal, ready to embrace the day with energy in the morning. The contrast with an alternative evening, where stress is avoided by merely sitting in a comfortable armchair with a glass of wine and some chips in front of the television, is remarkable. This could end with fatigue and the last memory of news, often saturated with global suffering and the possibility of negative nightmares.

The choice between these two scenarios seems clear. If more people agreed with me, concert halls would be bustling with visitors, and musicians would have much more work. Perhaps concert funding could even be supported by healthcare? Wouldn't that be a great idea? If I could demonstrate to our decision-makers that music helps reduce healthcare costs, wouldn't that be a win-win situation?

Or is returning to "real life" actually an escape from what we truly desire—relaxation, joy, and happiness? Could these be our birthrights, and are we inadvertently avoiding the only chance to embrace happiness? In this complex tangle of emotions, music seems to be our lifeline, offering us a chance to come home after a long quest for truth with our eyes firmly closed.

In the midst of my concerts, I feel like I'm extending an invitation to the audience—an invitation to escape and find their way back home. The healing that occurs is profound, a relief for the soul. Healing, not in the sense of miraculous cures, but in the restoration of normalcy. A return to a harmonious homeostasis where the body harmoniously blends with the soul, mind, and emotions. Even the cognitive brain, normally tangled in the cacophony of life, finds a moment of rest. The roles played by our minds, exhausted by a lifetime of fear-driven and worry-fueled addictive thoughts, finally come to a halt.

Music seems to be the vessel through which we navigate life's storm. It offers an opportunity to untangle tightly knotted lines, much like a ship preparing for a storm. In this harmonious journey, music becomes the only thread—the melody that untangles the knots, allowing us to return not as strangers but as rediscovered souls in harmony with the symphony of life.

In the enchanting sounds of the concert, the notes are released like beams of light dancing from a galactic tale, reminiscent of the dazzling brilliance of Star Wars. Each musical accent traverses emotional waves, weaving through space and filling every crevice of the hall, like warm breaths on wood and gentle caresses on seats and fabric carpets. An invisible glow, like luminous energy, embraces the audience.

The tones, as messengers of a timeless dimension, carry information embedded in an atmosphere where past and future merge. A realm of eternal knowledge that escapes our senses, but deep down, we know it exists. The sense of bliss woven into the melodies is a poetic testament to this transcendental experience. Through a mysterious passage, the sounds reach the soul, serving as a healing balm, soothing all disturbance, and like an artistic hand, smoothing the folds of the energetic fabric.

In this enchanting harmony, though it is not a panacea for all of life's issues, we find a source of rejuvenation. As the music flows through our energy channels like a benevolent breeze, disruptions awaken like dormant sparks, stimulated by the powerful frequencies of melodies. It is an internal movement of well-being, where our body, like a sculpture of emotions, gradually takes shape within the resonance of the musical universe. Observing this harmony is like having a different perspective, an inner knowledge that transcends the rational horizon, much like a poetic narrative in the language of sounds and vibrations. This mystery, akin to the incomprehensible wonders of yesteryears, now unfolds in the magic of the present moment.

Recalling my physics class, a crucial definition comes to mind: energy cannot be created or destroyed; it is an eternal force that has existed since the dawn of time and will endure indefinitely. However, this constant is not without change, as energy can transform into different forms. A striking example of this metamorphosis occurs in the ritual of burning wood. As the wood seems to sacrifice its warmth to the flames, the cycle reveals a deeper truth. The energy released during the combustion of wood breaks down into particles that float in the air, serving as nutrients for emerging trees.

These particles contribute to the grand biogeochemical story of Earth. CO_2, one of these particles, is absorbed by plants during photosynthesis, and then it navigates through the ecosystem. Water vapor contributes to cloud formation and precipitation, while other by-products undergo the alchemy of natural processes in the atmosphere.

The same fundamental approach to energy can be applied to the world of music. It is possible that the notes finding their way from our instruments are not merely auditory impressions; they represent a potential energy that does not abruptly stop after the last sound. Instead, this energy completes a cyclical journey, with the sounds spreading through the atmosphere resonating with the listener's sensitive strings through a subtle harmony. Just as the combustion process displays a continuous transformation of energy, music also releases an infinite flow of energy that extends beyond the physical perception of sound.

Amid the intoxicating symphonies of a live concert, the

audience discovers an enchanting dimension of musical richness. A fascinating aspect is revealed when exploring the profound complexity of frequencies, which manifests only in the presence of "real" instruments, far from the constraints of compressed recordings on CDs or mp3 files. In this mysterious realm, where each note whispers a story that transcends the audible limits, the soul is caressed by an invisible force.

Contemplating the infinite range of sound frequencies in a single note, our human perception can grasp only a fraction of this cosmic sound. It is a whirlpool of frequencies resonating in the atmosphere, a dance of sound waves that penetrates deeply into the emotional fibers of the listener. Like a sunset painting the sky with a palette of colors, live music illuminates the senses with a range of sounds, where each nuance tells a captivating story to enchant the listener.

In this living work of sound, live music transcends the limitations of compressed recordings and becomes a source of unfiltered emotions. It is a meeting with the unknown, where each note sparkles like a star in the sky, illuminating the darkness with its unique frequency. The ability of live concerts to envelop the listener in a tapestry of sounds, free from the digital reduction that recordings undergo, transforms each performance into a journey through the cosmos of sound.

In exploring sound, we encounter the intriguing parallel with the natural communication of animals. Dogs, whales and dolphins, whose auditory horizons extend beyond our own, weave their own symphonies in the silence of nature. Whales, the cosmopolitans of the ocean, share information about plankton locations over vast distances. Dolphins, regarded as the philosophers of the sea, communicate with refined signals that challenge human understanding.

The consciousness of live music embraces this harmony of nature, where frequencies blend like converging rivers in an ocean of sounds. It is an enchanting experience that moves the soul and transports the heart, a journey through a sonic landscape that can only be revealed live. Thus, concerts become not just performances but poetic journeys where the listener is invited to explore the unknown depths of sound and unravel the hidden meaning of each note.

In the realm of human consciousness during live concerts, as woven by the brilliant philosopher Carl Jung, the concept of the collective unconscious emerges as an intriguing thread that connects us all. Jung proposed that deep within the human psyche lies a reservoir of shared experiences, symbols and archetypes, which he called the collective unconscious. This fundamental layer of humanity, deeper than individual consciousness, forms the seed of universal themes found in mythologies, dreams, and cultural expressions.

A remarkable manifestation of this collective unconscious comes to life in the world of live music. Here, in the vibrant air of a concert hall or an outdoor stage, not only sound is produced, but also a shared emotional resonance that permeates all participants. It is an experience that, like an invisible thread, connects each individual in a common wave of human emotion.

Jung's archetypes, the primordial images emerging from the collective unconscious, seem to dance to the sounds of live music. The heroic journey, the struggle between light and darkness, love conquering all—these universal stories become tangible in the musical sounds that touch the soul. It is as if music, as a language of emotions, speaks directly to the deeply rooted archetypes in our collective being.

A live concert can be seen as a ritual, a communal experience where the boundaries between the individual self and the collective whole blur. The pulsating beat and moving melodies serve as anchors that take the individual listener on a journey that is not only personal but also part of a larger narrative we all share.

In the collective consciousness of a concert hall, not only the sounds of the music resonate but also the shared emotions and reactions of the audience. The euphoric outbursts, the silent emotional moments, the collective holding of breath during a breathtaking passage—these are moments when the collective consciousness comes alive and builds a bridge between individuals.

Live music becomes a powerful means of experiencing and exploring the collective unconscious. It is as if music opens the floodgates to deeper layers of our shared human essence, where the boundaries of self fade and we feel one with each other. In this shared sonic journey, a collective experience unfolds that is not only musical but also spiritual, reminding us of the invisible threads that connect us all in the rich tapestry of human existence.

To conclude this chapter, I would like to share a special experience I had with the greatest jazz violinist of all time, Stéphane Grappelli. As a young adult, I was captivated by his virtuosity, harmony, and exquisite musical talent. He never seemed to play a misplaced musical phrase. His records and concerts were always characterized by the most beautiful and delicate violin sounds imaginable. His playing included elegant, graceful lines, never forced or dramatic. There was never a wrong note or a clumsy fix of what is sometimes called a "hiccup," where a note is nearly played off-key. I considered him my mentor and role model, spending days replaying his solos, hoping to stand beside him one day. That dream truly came true when, after a long journey together, Stéphane invited me to perform a concert with him. Stéphane was my spiritual father. He never wanted to give me violin lessons; his lessons were more philosophical in nature. I could absorb his words when he gave me advice, almost disappointed by the simplicity of his discourse when it came to deep questions about playing, interpreting, and sharing music with the audience.

One day, Stéphane answered the most important question I

had ever asked him, a question that would influence my musical life. He said: "I never really had the ambition to be a pioneering innovator in the world of jazz. Although many consider me the father of jazz violin, my sole intention has always been to provide the audience with an enjoyable evening." At that moment, I didn't fully grasp the depth of his lesson, hidden behind the simple words of someone who truly shaped jazz violin. Nevertheless, those words have stayed with me, and even now, their echo resonates in my memory. It's not about us; it doesn't matter what we need to feed our ego. It's about what we can do to make the audience feel good during a performance. We don't need to want to invent something new; it's not necessary to reinvent music intellectually each time. I believe that throughout history, every possible note has already been played. We serve the music. We are the servants of nourishment for the human soul, providing what it needs to get the right nutrients and offer a bit of help in the quest through the meanders of life.

CHAPTER 4

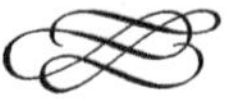

THE POWER OF SILENCE

In the infinite sea of sounds and rhythms that surround the world, we often overlook the crucial importance of silence as an instrument in the art of musical expression. Let us delve deeper into the enchantment of the interaction between silence and music, where silence is not merely the absence of sound but also the canvas upon which the most refined forms of musical expression take shape.

When we traditionally think of music, the idea of sound dominates our thoughts. Melodies, harmonies, and rhythms form the building blocks of what we consider to be music. However, this chapter invites us to see silence as a partner to sound, a collaborator that allows for the nuances and depths of musical expression. It encourages us to view it as a musical canvas painted with brushstrokes.

Silence, far from being empty, is presented as a fertile ground where the seeds of creative expression take root. It is the space between notes where the true magic of music unfolds. In these moments of silence, the sounds of previous notes still resonate, while the anticipation of what is to come holds the attentive ear. Here, silence is not simply seen as a pause between notes but rather as a living entity that gives music space to breathe and invites the listener into a contemplative dialogue with the sound.

By embracing silence as an integral part of musical expression, the listener is encouraged to look beyond the surface of sound. It is no longer merely a resting point; it becomes an active participant in the creative process. Silence acts as a subtle fabric that connects the diverse elements of a composition, creating a harmony that extends beyond audible tones.

This perspective on silence opens the door to a more intimate and profound experience of music. It invites the listener to experience silence as a powerful force that enhances the emotional impact of sound. Instead of merely listening to the sound, we are invited to listen to the space between the sounds, to the silence that carries and defines the notes.

You have probably experienced such a moment, where you were sitting with a group of friends or family in a charming café, somewhere in the heart of a bustling city like Paris or Barcelona. Imagine the narrow streets, adorned with colorful facades and cobblestone sidewalks, coming alive under the warm light of street lamps. The sound of animated conversation and laughter blends with the soft notes of live music emanating from nearby bars and restaurants.

You found a table on a cozy terrace, surrounded by blooming plants and ambient lighting. The aroma of freshly brewed coffee and delicious dishes fills the air, tantalizing your senses and awakening your appetite. The atmosphere is relaxed yet vibrant, and you look forward to an evening full of pleasure and camaraderie.

As you enjoy each other's company and the lively ambiance around you, a sudden silence falls over your group. The hustle and bustle of the busy streets seems to fade, and a peaceful calm descends upon your gathering. In these precious moments of silence, you feel a deep connection and mutual understanding, even without exchanging words.

"An angel is passing by," murmurs one of you, the voice soft yet penetrating. The others nod, aware of the meaning behind this expression. It's as if time stands still, and you are carried away by the sense of silence that envelops you.

The Power of Silence in Communication is often underestimated. "An angel is passing by" captures the dynamics of words, and in conversations, silence sometimes seems like a forgotten partner, an angel passing unnoticed amid the noise of spoken language. We now explore the subtlety and power of silence in communication, where the French expression "il y a un ange qui passe" sets the tone for the depth of meaning that can be attributed to silence.

"Il y a un ange qui passe." This expression, often used in French-speaking cultures, captures the unique atmosphere created when a moment of silence falls into a conversation. It suggests that there is something sacred in silence, as if an angel were listening attentively to what is being said. It reminds us that silence does not always mean emptiness; it can be a source of meaning and contemplation.

When a deliberate pause is introduced into a speech, the world seems momentarily suspended. Listeners, surprised by this unexpected void, are naturally drawn to the center of attention. It's as if the speaker is saying, "Pay attention, something important is happening." Silence acts as a frame for the words that follow, making them more impactful and memorable.

In an educational setting, the deliberate incorporation of extended silences can be a powerful tool. As students are accustomed to the constant flow of information and instruction, a sudden silence creates a moment of reflection. The teacher expresses: "Let's pause and absorb the information." Silence becomes a learning tool, allowing students to naturally calm down and open up to what comes next.

The impact of deliberately inserted silences in communication is most remarkable in public speaking. A well-placed silence can deepen the meaning of words, intensify emotions, and captivate the audience's attention. It's as if the speaker, by remaining silent, creates space for listeners to absorb, contemplate, and feel.

Thus, silence is an instrument of meaning, an angel passing by and inviting us to listen more deeply. Inserted into a speech, a classroom, or as a conscious choice in conversation, silence has the power to connect, deepen, and amplify the impact of communication.

Just as in conversations and everyday life, we also find this power in the world of music. Consider the rests in a musical piece, where the notes seem to take a brief pause before continuing. These musical silences serve not only as a breath for performers but also have a deeper meaning for listeners. It is in these moments of silence that musical phrases mature, and the emotions of the music are felt more intensely.

In jazz improvisation, for example, a silence between two notes can be as powerful as the notes themselves. It is a moment of tension and anticipation, where the listener waits to see what comes next. Such a silence can enrich the listening experience and reinforce the musical message, similar to how deliberate pauses function in spoken language.

Furthermore, parallels can be drawn with the world of contemporary pop music. Some of the most memorable songs contain moments of silence that create a dramatic effect. It's as if musicians momentarily freeze time to allow listeners to connect with the essence of the lyrics or melody.

In summary, just as in spoken language and other forms of expression, silence plays a crucial role in music. It is a powerful tool that deepens artistic messages, creates tension, and enriches the listening experience. In conversations and musical compositions, the deliberate use of silence is an art that exploits the subtlety of meaning and expression.

In the realm of compositions and improvisations, the value of silence is often underestimated. When I focus entirely on the silence, it feels as though a magical door opens, through which notes flow to me, like gentle whispers from the musical universe. The void between tones seems filled with a hidden melody waiting to be discovered. By dedicating all my attention to the silence, a deeper connection with the essence of the music emerges. The notes do not just emanate from my instrument; they seem to resonate with the silence itself, creating a unique harmony that extends beyond audible sounds. It is a subtle play between the audible and the inaudible, where silence acts as a fertile ground on which musical expression thrives and comes to life. Understanding and appreciating this relationship between silence and music opens the door to a deeper and more satisfying musical experience.

At times, I find myself doubting my role in composing the piece. It feels as though an elusive entity, an additional dimension, guides me through the musical journey. I realize that each improvisation is unique, and I doubt whether I could play the same melody again, as if there were a creative force constantly exploring new paths. In these moments of musical exploration, silence is not just the absence of sound; it is rather the passage to an infinite space of possibilities where notes manifest as unexpected guides. This sense of guided improvisation reinforces my belief that the relationship between silence and music anticipates our understanding, opening the door to a creative process that extends beyond the individual self.

Several renowned composers and musicians have embraced the depth of silence and meditation as a source of creative inspiration. A notable figure in this regard is John Cage, an American composer who pushed the boundaries of experimental music. His most emblematic work, *4'33"*, consists of four minutes and thirty-three seconds during which musicians deliberately produce no sound, prompting the audience to pay attention to ambient noises and recognize the value of silence as an essential part of musical expression.

A similar approach is found in the work of British composer John Tavener, whose compositions are imbued with contemplative and sacred elements. Inspired by his spiritual practices and meditative reflections, Tavener consciously explores silence to discover new ideas, drawing from the serene source of creativity. Together, these examples highlight the importance of silence as fertile ground for exploring new musical possibilities and nurturing the creative process.

Throughout the history of music, the recognition of silence as an artistic medium has manifested in various ways. The Flemish polyphony, a school of composers from the 15th and 16th centuries, made significant contributions to this concept. In compositions by figures such as Guillaume Dufay and Josquin des Prez, the emphasis was not only on the complexity of polyphony but also on the space between the notes, where silence emerged as a dynamic force.

The sacred nature of these polyphonic works, often composed for religious ceremonies, reinforced the idea of silence as a spiritually charged element. It was not merely an absence of sound but rather a poetic pause inviting the listener to contemplation. The musical silence served as a breath between celestial harmonies, a moment where the soul could resonate with the divine.

Even in later periods, such as the Romantic era, the composer Anton Bruckner sought the expressive power of silence in his sacred compositions, such as masses and symphonies. He created moments of stillness to guide the listener toward a deeper understanding of the divine mystery imbued in his music.

The French composer Claude Debussy once said, "Music is

the space between the notes." This underscores the importance of pauses, how they shape the musical landscape, and allow for storytelling. When we play music, we continuously navigate between sound and silence, and it is this interaction that makes music vibrant and dynamic.

Flemish polyphonists and later composers recognized that silence was not just a void but a vibrant space where meaning could flourish. They invited listeners to view silence not merely as the absence of sound but as an active and transformative force within the musical experience.

I recall during the recording of Béla Bartók's 44 Duos, a shared adventure with my musical partner Marco Ambrosini, we reached a critical stage late into the night. Marco was applying the masterful final touches as the darkness awaited the dawn of a new day. At that hour, tired but filled with musical energy, another challenge awaited me. Marco, absorbed in the final touch, suggested that I establish the new order of the pieces. Béla Bartók had indicated on his scores that they could be rearranged at will. It was 5 a.m., and despite the fatigue, I let my thoughts rest in the surrounding silence. In an instant, the notes flowed naturally from my pen without hesitation. Marco reacted with admiration, and later, after a well-deserved rest, the order proved to be nothing short of perfect. It almost seemed as if Bartók himself, though invisible, had imprinted his mark on the sequence composition through my hands. In homage to the master, we considered adding a photo to the CD cover, a moment where we raised a triple toast to the successful conclusion of our musical adventure, including an extra glass symbolizing that Bartók himself, though invisible, had participated in our triumph.

We can also view silence as a prelude to music. In the theater of musical performances, silence is often the gateway to magic. It is a moment of introspection, where the audience, filled with anticipation and silence, holds its breath awaiting the sonic journey ahead. It is the essence of the calm before the storm, a moment charged with promise.

When the hall is filled with silent anticipation, the silence itself resonates as a work of art. The musician, enveloped in the serene atmosphere of silence, stands on the threshold of creation. It is a timeless moment where the notes have yet to be played but already linger in the air, waiting to come to life. The space is imbued with an almost palpable tension, a silence that connects age-old tranquility with musical expression.

The conductor, as the alchemist of sound, stands before the musicians and immerses the hall in a silence rich with meaning. It is a delicate, wordless conversation between the conductor and the orchestra, a moment where silence serves as the backdrop against which the first sketches of musical splendor will emerge. The conductor, guardian of this precious silence, waits a brief moment before opening the invisible door to the world of sound.

This fleeting silence, charged with anticipation, holds the potential for the unexpected. The audience, closely linked to the musician and conductor through the power of silence, is taken on a journey that extends beyond audible sounds. It is an experience that embraces the depth of musical expression, a shared moment of silence that lays the foundation for the forthcoming harmony.

A connection is forged between the artist and the audience. It is a shared understanding of the moment, a silence that speaks and leaves resonances that extend beyond the final note. Thus, silence becomes an intimate dialogue between the musician, the conductor and the audience. It is in this silence that the soul of the music is felt, where sound and silence intertwine to tell a captivating story together.

When I step onto the stage, a deep sense of calm envelops my being. It is a moment saturated with concentration, an inner silence that I cherish and consciously cultivate. Before taking the stage, I seek the tranquility of my dressing room, where I meditate. I carry this serene atmosphere with me onto the stage.

Every step I take, every foot that touches the stage, is imbued with intention. It is more than just physical contact; it is a grounding ritual. Feeling my feet absorb the vibrant energy of the stage is grounding me in the present. The stage becomes not only a physical space but also a sacred realm where silence and anticipation merge.

In these moments of connection with the stage, I allow myself to be guided by the power of my meditation. It is an intimate dance with silence, where every movement, every breath, is imbued with awareness. As I carry my inner calm into the spotlight, silence becomes my companion, an invisible partner in this musical adventure.

The atmosphere of the audience, like a living entity, becomes tangible. I inhale the anticipation, sensing curiosity floating in the air. It is a play between silence and shared anticipation. Silence acts as a bridge connecting the audience and me, a subtle fabric filling the space between us.

Thus, the stage becomes a sacred meeting place. In the silence, I prepare to tell my musical story, and in those serene moments before the first note, I feel a deep resonance with the present audience. It is not just a performance; it is a shared experience, born from silence and carried by the sounds that follow. The silence of the stage becomes an opening, a doorway to a world rich with expression and connection, where each note resonates with the echo of the inner calm that preceded entry into this sacred space.

When I let the first note resonate, I feel a profound connection with my instrument. The silence, which had previously left the audience in anticipation, is now filled with sounds imbued with concentration and intention. Between each note, attention seems to float, a delicate thread connecting the musical phrases. I don't just hear the sounds flowing from my violin; I also sense the space between them, a living fabric carrying the music.

I ride on waves of sound, carried by harmonies and melodies intertwining in the air. My violin becomes an extension of my deepest emotions, and the silence remains as a canvas on which my musical expression comes to life. In these moments, I am not just a musician but also a participant in a ritual where silence and sound blend into an enchanting experience.

The intensity of this phenomenon is further heightened when I am surrounded by fellow musicians resonating on the same wavelength. Like a collective breath, we follow the silences and fill them with harmonies, seamlessly blending into one another. Together, we weave a symphony of silence, where every musical nuance is carried by the collective concentration of the ensemble.

In this shared silence we discover a common language, a subtle dialogue unfolding between the notes. We sense each other without words, understand each other's sonic nuances, and anticipate the silences as if we were a single entity. It's a unique connection that emerges when individual musical voices merge into a collective masterpiece.

The concentration I feel between the notes also blends with the focus of my fellow musicians, creating an atmosphere where music and silence go hand in hand. It's a shared journey through sound and silence, where the space between the notes becomes as important as the notes themselves. It's in these moments that the magic of music reveals itself fully, like a collective meditation where the boundaries between individual expression and collective harmony blur.

Similarly, during musical performances, I discover how the meaning and depth of the music are revealed in the intervening silences. At these moments, sounds, like words in a conversation, reveal their full meaning in the spaces between the notes. These intervening silences serve as the breath of musical language, allowing the music to be not only heard but also understood on a deeper level.

In my musical collaborations with others, I've learned that, just as in spoken language, it is essential to "read between the notes." This way, you capture not only the individual sounds but also the subtle nuances, emotions and hidden intentions between the notes. It's a form of listening that goes beyond the surface, akin to understanding the underlying meaning of spoken words by attentively listening to the silences between them.

This parallel between music and language illustrates how both art forms contain depth and richness in the intermediate spaces. Just as we often understand a conversation better by listening not only to the words but also to the pauses, we can uncover the true essence of music by paying attention to the silences between the notes. It is in these moments of shared silence that true communication occurs, where music is not just heard but also felt and understood.

In our exploration of the transformative power of silence, we have discovered not only how deeply it is woven into musical expression but also how it emerges as a healing force in other fields. One such field is biodynamic craniosacral osteopathy, where silence appears as the "still point"—a moment of total rest and harmony. In this therapeutic window, the body has the opportunity to recover, and silence serves as the key to unlocking well-being on a deeper level.

Parallel to this physical approach, in quantum physics we find the fascinating world of zero-point energy. In this apparent emptiness lies a treasure of potential energy, similar to the creative power that emerges between musical notes. Here, silence not only connects disciplines but also bridges the apparent dichotomy between void and abundance.

In the context of music, we can consider these various forms of silence as related. Just as silence in biodynamic craniosacral osteopathy brings healing and balance, silence in quantum physics functions as a reservoir of creative possibilities. This once again illustrates the versatility of silence as a transformative and connective force, playing a crucial role across various disciplines and revealing deep connections between science, medicine and art.

Meditation, in its different forms and traditions, offers a calm space where the tumult of thoughts settles. It is a process of awareness, a return to the present moment, and a conscious slowing of the mind. Meditation allows for a deeper connection with oneself, which is essential for emotional well-being.

Music, on the other hand, is a universal language that can express emotions and feelings often not captured by words. Vibrations and sounds have the ability to penetrate deeply into the soul and create emotional resonance. Alongside meditation, music can be a powerful tool for exploring and healing the inner landscape.

By incorporating meditation practices while listening to music, concentration is intensified and a deeper connection with the sounds is established. The ability of music to evoke emotions and the practice of meditation to consciously experience those emotions create a beneficial synergy for the mind and body.

Some people choose to combine guided meditations with specific musical genres, instruments, or sound frequencies to create a personalized experience. The slow and contemplative movements of meditation can be synchronized with the rhythms and melodies of music, leading to profound harmony.

In the realm of meditative music, genres such as ambient, new age, and certain forms of classical music have found their place in healing practices. Artists compose pieces with the intention of creating an atmosphere of serenity and relaxation, thus facilitating listeners' easier entry into meditative states.

In the rich symphony of life, nature resonates as a masterful composer, and its silence forms the resting point between the notes of the endless song. This natural silence, deeply intertwined with the sounds of rustling leaves, babbling brooks, and gentle movements of animals, finds its reflection in the art of music. The parallels between the silence of nature and the silence in compositions reveal not only the versatility of silence as an artistic tool but also as a universal principle shared across different disciplines.

In the world of music, silence is not merely seen as the absence of sound but rather as a powerful instrument to accentuate emotions and give meaning to sound. Composers find their inspiration in the natural symphonies around them. A light breeze in the leaves becomes a delicate violin melody, while the flow of a brook can determine the rhythmic pulse of a piece. The silence between these natural sounds is not considered a void but rather a stage on which the composers choreographs their own masterpieces.

Natural silence and silence in music together form a subtle fabric that connects different aspects of life. They illustrate how silence is not simply a pause between notes but a force that penetrates deeply into human experience. Whether it is the tranquility of a wooded path or the striking silence between the sounds of a symphony, silence remains a timeless companion in the melody of life.

The concept of silence is beautifully embodied in the Japanese tradition of "Ma", a term that describes the space between objects, the emptiness that gives meaning and depth to form. In Japanese culture, the concept of "Ma" is deeply rooted in art, architecture, and daily life. "Ma" is often translated as "space" or "pause," but these translations do not do justice to the richness of the concept.

"Ma" is not passive; it is an active void that influences the dynamics of a composition or a space. For example, in the architecture of Japanese gardens, the empty spaces between trees and rocks create a sense of tranquility and harmony, giving each element its own place and significance. In traditional Japanese music, as in the art of Noh theater, pauses and silences are just as important as the sounds themselves, achieving a deeper emotional impact.

This principle of "Ma" and the power of silence can also be applied to our daily lives. Just as in music, pauses and silences in our lives can help us find meaning, reflect, and establish deeper connections with ourselves and others. Embracing silence can help us be more present, to listen and feel instead of always doing and speaking.

Meditation is a practice closely related to the concept of "Ma." It involves finding peace and silence in the mind, creating space for inner calm and awareness. In music, this meditative approach can help us listen more deeply, be more present in the moment, and appreciate the subtle nuances of sound and silence. By focusing on our breath, the movements of our hands, and the resonance of each note, we cultivate a meditative concentration that leads to a richer and more meaningful musical experience, touching both the performer and the audience.

In the complex world of silence, a profound relationship exists between the power of intention and the significant silences that frame the notes. This symbiosis between intention and silence emerges as a crucial element in the art of composing, playing, and listening to music.

Intention, as an inner force that animates each note, serves as my compass. It is the inspiring force that infuses every vibration, shapes every melody, and directs every harmony. When I play with genuine intention, each note is imbued with meaning and emotion. Music speaks for itself, not merely as a series of sounds but as an expression of deeply felt intention.

However, when the space between the notes takes form, it is in these moments of silence that intention can fully manifest. Like a pause between phrases in a conversation, silence in music creates space for the listener to absorb and understand the deeper layers of intention.

In the realm of composition, the power of intention is visible in the choices I make. The motivation behind each note, each chord, and each silence contributes to the overall atmosphere of the piece. My clear intention perceives how to use silence as a backdrop against which the musical vision comes to life.

As a performing musician, my power of intention is palpable in every piece played. It is the inner fire that guides the fingers, controls the breath, and conveys emotion to the audience. Simultaneously, the silence between the notes becomes a stage on which intention can resonate and touch the listener on a deeper level.

In improvisation, a particularly remarkable phenomenon occurs when intention and silence converge. Here, I become an explorer, guided by an inner intention and surrounded by silence that allows for spontaneous creativity. I find that silence is not merely a void but rather a source of inspiration, a place where new ideas germinate.

The combination of the power of intention and silence in music reveals a profound truth: that music is not just sound but an expression of inner movements and contemplative pauses. In this harmony between intention and silence, a musical experience emerges that touches the soul and takes the listener on a journey beyond audible tones.

In the depths of silence, my authentic voice unfolds, giving birth to originality. It is in these calm moments, where the tumult of the world fades, that I can find myself and develop a unique musical identity. Originality in music is reflected not only in compositions but also in improvisations and performances, originating from the deepest core of oneself.

Originality in music is not a quest for the unknown but rather a return to myself. It is a recognition of my own voice amid the sound universe. In silence, I find the courage to be authentic, to sing my own melody, to create my own harmonies, and to embrace my own rhythms. Thus, music becomes not only a form of art but also a manifestation of the deepest truth of our personality.

In silence, I find an infinite reservoir of inspiration. It is a source that never runs dry, a continuous flow of creative energy that unfolds when I am ready to listen to its whispers. Unlike the daunting writer's block in the literary world, silence offers an uninterrupted and inexhaustible stream of creative impulses.

The seemingly paradoxical nature of silence is evident in its ability to speak without words. It is a fertile ground where the seeds of creativity germinate. By immersing myself in this silence, I do not experience a lack of ideas; on the contrary, I am inundated with a multitude of melodies, harmonies, and rhythms waiting to be discovered and expressed.

The phenomenon of writer's block, which sometimes afflicts composers and authors, stopping them from putting pen to paper, can be overcome by the magic of silence. When I am willing to let external noise fade and allow internal silence to emerge, the concept of creative blockage disappears. Instead, I become a channel for an apparently endless flow of melodies and harmonies.

Silence offers an infinite source of variation and nuance. It is like a palette of colors from which I can choose an inexhaustible stock of sound possibilities. Here, each silence between the notes becomes an opportunity to discover something new, to experiment with the blending of sounds and emotions.

This infinite source of inspiration is not limited to specific genres or styles. In classical compositions, jazz improvisations, or experimental soundscapes, silence offers an unlimited playground where musicians can explore and create. It is a constant companion, always present, ready to reveal new musical worlds.

In conclusion, in silence I discover not only the depth of my own creative potential but also an inexhaustible source of inspiration that continues to nourish me throughout my artistic journey as a musician and in my passion for creating bronze sculptures.

In the depths of silence, I realize that the present moment is the only one that truly exists. This moment, the Now, is the timeless essence in which all creation occurs. It is a consciousness that guides me through each note, each pause, and each breath pattern.

At a turning point in my musical journey, when I was 25, my violin teacher introduced me to a source of inspiration that would transform my understanding of music and life: the writings of Jiddu Krishnamurti. This introduction to the philosophy of the "Moment" opened the door to a deeper perception of silence, creativity, and the inevitable Now.

Krishnamurti, a wise and visionary thinker, approached life with radical simplicity. His teachings invite a direct confrontation with the reality of the moment, a concept that would later play a crucial role in my musical expression. According to Krishnamurti, the "Moment" is not an abstract philosophy but rather the immediate and direct experience of the present instant, without the intervention of the mind.

The impact of Krishnamurti's insights on my musical practice has been profound. He taught me to live the flow of my music without the constraints of preconceived ideas or expectations. In the silence of the Now, I found a space where my violin not only produced notes but became a vibrant expression of the moment itself.

With Krishnamurti as my guide, I discovered that silence is the very essence of creativity. Music, when born from the

"Moment," becomes a dynamic expression of life as it is, with no yesterday or tomorrow.

Simultaneously with my introduction to Krishnamurti's wisdom by my violin teacher, I continued to integrate his ideas into my musical practice. The moment I embrace my violin is infused with a consciousness that invites me to listen, play, and be in the timeless silence of the Now.

After my first encounter with Krishnamurti, my journey into the realm of silence further unfolded through encounters with a treasure of wise masters. These visionary guides nurtured my understanding of silence and taught me the subtle art of applying this power to my musical expression. Among them, some offered deeply penetrating insights.

Khalil Gibran, the Lebanese-American poet and philosopher, conveyed to me the poetic essence of silence. His words reached beyond the surface of sound and introduced me to the deeper layers of inner silence. In his philosophical works, I discovered that silence is not merely an external absence of sound but also an internal space where the soul can meet itself.

Sri Ramana Maharshi, the Indian spiritual master, opened my eyes to the transformative power of meditative silence. His teachings emphasized the importance of inner contemplation and how this silence can purify the mind, leading to a deeper understanding of oneself and the world. These ideas found their reflection in my approach to silence as an inner journey in music.

Sri Aurobindo, the Indian philosopher, added a dimension of spiritual evolution to my understanding of silence. His teachings on integrating spiritual forces into daily life were woven into my musical practice. Thus, I discovered that silence is not merely a resting point but also a catalyst for growth and transformation.

Eckhart Tolle, the contemporary spiritual teacher, brought the power of the "now" into my awareness. His emphasis on the present moment, free from mental noise, found its reflection in my approach to silence before, during, and after my musical expressions. The "now" became a living source of creativity and expression.

Each of these masters left a unique imprint of wisdom that deepened my understanding of silence and enriched my art. Their ideas were not abstract concepts but living principles that I have woven into my musical explorations. Thus, these masters, as silent guides in the background, continue to illuminate my journey with the timeless power of silence.

The journey through silence has not only infused my artistic practices but also triggered a profound change in every facet of my existence. Silence, once considered a companion of creative expression, has now nestled at the heart of my life, like an intimate movement of tranquility that shapes the rhythm of my days.

In my daily activities, intertwined with the demands of modern life, silence has unlocked an unexpected efficiency. As I prepare for a meeting, a conversation, or even a moment of rest, I listen to the inner silent space. This practice has enhanced my ability to respond from a place of inner calm, approaching the complexity of life with a clarity that was previously unknown.

It's as if silence, once integrated into my daily rituals, spreads its soothing wings over the turbulent waters of my experiences. It has tamed the storms of stress and sharpened the clarity of reflection. My life now unfolds in a natural rhythm, carried by the invisible waves of silence.

Silence is no longer confined to the moments before stepping onto the stage or beginning an artistic project. It is woven into the fabric of my relationships, work, and personal growth. As an omnipresent companion, silence guides me in my quest for understanding, compassion, and authenticity.

I am amazed by the profound transformation brought about by silence; it is the key to a deeper connection with life itself.

My journey through silence has enriched my artistic expressions, but more importantly, it has infused my entire existence with a fluid grace that anchors my heart and mind in peaceful harmony.

In the maze of decisions, where paths split into countless possibilities, silence has emerged as my trustworthy guide. Like an inner compass, silence points the way through the labyrinth of choices, an invisible hand guiding me through the complexity of life.

When making decisions, big or small, I seek silence. It's as if the answers to my questions lie dormant in the calm between my thoughts. In these moments of silence, clarity emerges, unmarred by the noise of the external world. Here, in the silent chambers of my mind, I find the space to listen to my deepest desires, my inner compass.

Even while writing this book, a new and challenging endeavor, silence has revealed its mysterious power. As I sit before the blank page, I listen and let the words unfold. Thus, creativity is born.

Silence also advises me in times of trouble. In the silent realm of my inner world, where judgment is absent, I can express my concerns and questions. Silence, like a wise friend, listens, understands, and helps me organize my thoughts to find a solution.

Silence is a companion in self-discovery, a reliable advisor. Thus, silence becomes not only an artistic tool but also an enlightened guide on my path of choice and creation.

Silence also allows me to let go. I realize that an invisible thread connects me to the universal fabric of life. This trust does not rely on words or visible proof, but rather on the gentle, calm whispers of silence itself.

In the silence, I learn that it's not about achieving the "right" outcome, but about the sincerity and intention with which I make my choices and walk my path. It's an awareness that every moment, even one that feels dark or challenging, is a milestone on my journey of growth and development.

Reminded that silence serves as an inner guide, I am part of a higher dimension. In this surrender, a deeper understanding of my own inner compass emerges, a compass fuelled by a silent force that dissolves all doubts.

This trust that arises from silence is like a gentle breeze filling the sails of my life's vessel. It is not a trust based on control or predictability, but rather on the realization that every change in course, every turn, is part of a greater plan that transcends my understanding.

A powerful sense of responsibility also awakens; a realization dawns on me like a gentle breeze, and I have no more excuses. Previously, external factors would lead me to make excuses in the face of my disappointments. But in silence, there is no room for denial. Silence makes me lucid about my choices.

Silence invites me to self-reflection, to ask questions that resonate deeply in my soul. What value do my experiences hold? How can I act more consciously? What are my deepest intentions? In these questions, a profound understanding emerges: Being responsible offers me a new perspective on life.

From being a victim, I become an active participant in the creative process of my existence. Silence acts as a mentor, urging me to embrace my power to shape my reality.

CHAPTER 5

HARMONIES OF INTERTWINED STRINGS: THE NYCKELHARPA

The nyckelharpa, an enchanting musical instrument rooted in Sweden's rich musical heritage, embodies a harmonious fusion of tradition, craftsmanship, and the timeless magic of music. The unique sound and distinctive appearance of the nyckelharpa embrace not only the soul of the musician but also that of the listener; it is a remarkable instrument.

The name "nyckelharpa," which literally means "key harp" or "keyed fiddle," comes from the keys or tangents placed on the instrument's strings. These tangents, when pressed, alter the pitch of the strings, allowing the musician to produce a wide range of tones. Although the instrument has undergone various developments over the centuries, it retains its characteristic appearance with a set of strings and a wooden keyboard.

The nyckelharpa reveals its magic not only in the played strings but also in the secret resonance of the sympathetic strings. Positioned beneath the bridge and sometimes above it, alongside the melodic strings, where the melody resonates, are apparently hidden sound treasures. These strings are not played directly but vibrate in subtle harmony, like silent companions responding to each played note.

With each note, a delicate interaction occurs with the corresponding sympathetic string, resonating in harmony. This invisible presence creates additional reverberation, an echo of the played melody that envelops the listener in an enchanting atmosphere. Each note opens a deeper dimension, a resonance extending beyond the immediate sound, weaving a subtle web of sounds in the air.

From this interplay of played and sympathetic strings emerges a unique sound world. The instrument transports listeners to hidden soundscapes and invites them to wander through mysterious resonances. It is a symphony of vibrations, a fusion of direct tones forming an enchanting musical fabric.

Historically, the nyckelharpa has deep roots in Scandinavian musical traditions dating back to the Middle Ages. It often served as an accompaniment to folk music and dances, enriching the melodies of festive gatherings and joyful celebrations. Curiously, the nyckelharpa also found its place in religious contexts, where it was used to accompany liturgical chants, demonstrating versatility beyond mere folk music.

The nyckelharpa, also known as the "viola d'amore a chiavi" in the world of baroque music, reveals its versatility through the centuries. Etymologically, the name does not come from "amore" (love), but from "the Moors." When the Catholics expelled the Moors from Spain and Portugal, they wanted to hide every reference to them, and thus the "violin of the Moors" became the "viola d'amore." By historical coincidence, the instrument received a name that refers to love, which I find fitting. With its sympathetic strings that resonate beneath the surface with the played melody, the viola d'amore offers a warm, velvety sound. Every note feels like a gentle embrace, infused with romance and deep emotion.

In the undulating melodies of the Sienaharpa from the medieval world of Guillaume de Machault, echoes of a rich musical heritage are found. The deep resonance of the nyckelharpa double bass, the refined sounds of the silverbasharpa, and the harmonious tones of the Moraharpa take us on a journey through ancient Sweden. Each instrument contributes to the colorful sound palette, woven into the infinite symphony of history.

The nyckelharpa has left its mark in the writings of music historians such as Martin Agricola and Michael Praetorius. In their works, imbued with the spirit of the Renaissance and the early baroque period, the nyckelharpa is praised as a unique instrument that enchants both the musician's and the listener's soul. These historical references shed intriguing light on its evolution and role in the musical landscapes of bygone times.

The technique of playing the nyckelharpa is one of its most striking features. With a bow, the musician caresses the strings, while the tangents are operated with the other hand. This unique approach to playing gives the nyckelharpa its own distinctive sound character. The tones are often vivid, resonant, and penetrating, forming a powerful expression of rich colors.

On a traditional violin, the fingers press directly on the strings to create the melody; a curious change occurs on the nyckelharpa. Here, it is the tangents that act as intermediaries between the fingers and the strings. These wooden keys serve as intermediaries, with the finger pressing on them, which in turn strike the string.

This particular approach gives the nyckelharpa a unique advantage. Due to the intervention of the tangents, the intonation, or the precision of each note, is almost inherent. The tangents serve as precise guides, ensuring the musician's fingers are in the exact position. The result is a smooth melody, where each note retains its purity, a characteristic that makes the instrument's enchanting sonic richness even more striking.

The nyckelharpa has experienced a remarkable revival and is no longer confined to the shadow of other more well-known string instruments. It has found its place on contemporary musical stages around the world, with modern musicians and composers exploring its possibilities and integrating it into various musical genres.

The uniqueness of the nyckelharpa goes beyond its sound alone. The instrument carries the heritage of generations of musicians and reflects the deep cultural roots of Sweden. The craftsmanship behind making a nyckelharpa is itself an art, combining traditional methods and materials with contemporary techniques. The resulting instrument is not only a musical tool but also a work of art that tells the stories of its creators.

In the skilled hands of a player, the nyckelharpa becomes a gateway to emotion and imagination, capable of conveying joy, melancholy, and everything in between. Its ability to be both playful and profound makes it suitable for a wide range of musical expressions. Whether performing the lively melodies of a Swedish folk dance, being part of a contemporary musical experience, or accompanying chants in a religious setting, the nyckelharpa remains an instrument that transcends the boundaries of time and tradition.

As a living monument to musical heritage and creativity, the nyckelharpa continues to be a source of inspiration and wonder. Its modest appearance hides a treasure trove of sounds and stories, making it a remarkable chapter in the world of music.

In our journey through the pages of this book, I have already introduced the concept of the "violin" as a recurring motif. However, it is important to understand that when I refer to the violin, I am delving into a realm that extends beyond the conventional instrument we are familiar with. The term encompasses a rich soundscape that delves into the mystical depths of the nyckelharpa. Thus, when you encounter mentions of the violin, let yourself be guided by the musical threads woven throughout this narrative, where the nyckelharpa, akin to a related spirit, intertwines its melodies with those of its classical counterpart. In this harmonious fusion of sounds and meanings, the distinctions between the instruments blur, heralding a symphony of musical revelations that transcend the confines of the traditional violin. Let us embark together on this musical exploration, where the violin serves not only as an instrument but also as a poetic bridge to the diverse sonic realms of the nyckelharpa.

In the fabric of the universe, where sounds and vibrations converge like particles of dust in a sunbeam, the mystery of sympathetic resonances unfolds. Science and poetry converge in this enchanting phenomenon, where the invisible strings of existence are touched by the vibrations of sound.

Sympathetic resonance, in scientific terms, is the phenomenon where an object begins to vibrate or resonate in response to the vibrations of another, nearby object. A simple example from everyday life: imagine a bus speeding by, causing the windows of nearby buildings to vibrate. This is an invisible conversation between materials, where the vibrations of the bus are captured and responded to by the surrounding structures.

A more sublime example of sympathetic resonance is found in the world of music. Imagine a soprano whose voice reaches the highest pitches. When she hits the perfect note, a nearby glass may start to vibrate. This is not just a theatrical spectacle but a manifestation of the physical principles of sympathetic resonance. The glass "recognizes" the frequency of the note and responds with a potential shattering.

The nyckelharpa, this enchanting Swedish musical instrument with its keys and strings, forms a link in this story of resonance. As a bridge between the scientific and artistic worlds, the nyckelharpa possesses a cathedral-like sound that resonates with the deepest fibers of the human being. Its tones, like prayers rising towards the vaults of the universe, seek harmony between the material and spiritual worlds.

A fascinating parallel appears with resonance in religious contexts. Imagine the sounds rising during liturgical chants, where the vibrations of the nyckelharpa fill the space and create an atmosphere of transcendence. The keys of the instrument become ritualistic keys that open the door to a dimension where sound is not only heard but also felt deep within the heart.

These examples of sympathetic resonance remind us that the universe is imbued with a hidden harmony. It is a symphony where the vibrations of one object speak to the silence of another, and where sound is not just an isolated event but a journey through the very resonances of existence.

In this enchanting dance of sounds and vibrations, emerges a space where science and poetry go hand in hand. Sympathetic resonances invite us to listen to the deeper resonances of life, where sound is not a mere chance occurrence but a mysterious expression of hidden harmony.

Among the rich array of musical instruments, we find many companions to the nyckelharpa, each with its own unique resonances and enchanting sound worlds. One such deeply rooted instrument from Indian traditions is the sarangi. With its characteristic resonant strings, this instrument produces a deep and expressive sound. It seems like a storyteller painting an emotional palette with each vibration, captivating listeners in a musical odyssey.

The sitar is also part of this family of resonance. With its elongated neck and sympathetic strings resonating with every stroke, it creates a sound imbued with ancient traditions. The resonances, like echoes of the past, add depth to each note, creating an enchanting soundscape. The listener is transported to mystical worlds.

This family of intertwined stringed instruments reveals a universal truth: resonance is the language of music, penetrating the soul of listeners. Each instrument, with its unique resonances, contributes to the rich tapestry of sounds that populate the musical world. Like a Star Wars laser beam, the vibrations of all these instruments traverse space, reaching the receptive ears of the audience. It is a harmonic spectacle where frequencies, like magical particles, float in the air, finding their way into the hearts of listeners.

A fascinating experiment with two 440 Hz tuning forks sheds special light on the world of resonance and the power of similar frequencies. When one tuning fork is struck and brought close to a second tuning fork of the same frequency, something remarkable happens. Without direct contact, the frequencies of the first fork transfer to the second.

This phenomenon illustrates the principle of sympathetic resonance, where two objects with similar natural frequencies respond to each other. The tuning forks are, in a sense, "harmonized" with each other, a delicate dance of vibrations that is invisible but palpable. It is a metaphor for the power of equal frequencies finding each other, an interaction that occurs not only in the world of musical instruments but also in the broader spectrum of our existence. This phenomenon also reflects the power of similar frequencies in the world of music.

Considering all this, the phenomenon extends to our daily lives, where similar frequencies generate resonances in our emotions, thoughts, and even in the spaces we inhabit.

When the nyckelharpa is not properly tuned, the sympathetic strings do not produce harmonious resonances; instead, they can even become disruptive. This delicate balance between the played strings and the sympathetic strings is crucial to creating the unique sound world of the nyckelharpa. This sensitive gateway to a magical dimension only opens when all components are harmoniously tuned.

Beyond the perfect tuning of the nyckelharpa itself, another crucial factor contributes to revealing its enchanting sounds: the tuning of the musician. Harmony between the musician and the instrument is essential for a captivating performance.

Metaphorically, musicians must be tuned from within, in

harmony with their own emotions, thoughts, and physical condition. When musicians achieve an emotional equilibrium, they can then bring out the deeper resonances of their instrument. It is a synergy between the sound world of the instrument and the inner world of the player, where each note reflects the artist's emotional state.

But it goes further. To create a truly magical concert, the musician must also be able to "tune" the audience. Here, not only does the music matter, but also the interaction, the shared energy between the stage and the audience. The musician acts as a tuning fork, emitting resonances that influence the audience. This process of tuning requires subtlety and intuition, with the musician sensing the atmosphere in the room and adjusting their performance to establish a deeper connection.

The perfect tuning of a musical instrument is essential, and a successful concert requires a similar tuning, though on an emotional and social level. It is this delicate balance between the musician, the instrument and the audience that allows for a harmonious performance, in which the nyckelharpa reveals its full potential and captivates listeners with its unique sound palette.

The phenomenon of "good vibes" and "bad vibes" resembles an invisible symphony that we perceive as soon as we enter a space. Just like musical instruments, our environments are also imbued with a subtle energy that our senses immediately pick up.

When we enter a space, we instinctively feel the atmosphere it reveals. We pick up on the vibrations of emotions, interactions, and the energy saturating the space. A recent argument may still be palpable, like a dissonant note that continues to resonate. Similarly, joy, love, and harmony can manifest as a warm and inviting sound. If we are aware of these "vibes," we can try to contribute to a positive harmony, much like musicians carefully tune their instruments for a performance.

In a way, we act as walking nyckelharpas, with the ability to harmonize our own vibrations with the world around us. It's a reminder of the power we have, not only to influence our own mood but also the tone of the spaces we inhabit. It's an invitation to consciously choose a symphony of positive resonance, knowing that our "vibes" are a powerful instrument in creating a harmonious melody in daily life.

In the deepest fabric of our existence, not only do our organs, bones and muscles vibrate at specific frequencies, but each thought also has its own subtle harmony. The complex symphony of the human body and mind is revealed by scientific instruments like EEG scanners, which, like a musical score, can map the frequencies of our thoughts.

Our brains, as conductors of this inner symphony, release a set of electrical impulses corresponding to different states of consciousness. Delta frequencies during deep sleep, theta frequencies during meditation or dreaming, alpha waves that appear during relaxation, beta waves that dominate during active alertness, and finally, faster gamma waves involved in cognitive processes—each forms a unique melody of our mental state.

Just as a nyckelharpa depends on precise tuning to produce its full sound, our inner orchestra also requires careful tuning of thoughts. Negative thoughts resonate like dissonant notes, while positive thoughts form a harmonious chord. The art of tuning our thoughts is essential, not only for our own well-being but also for the atmosphere we create around us.

The power of positive thinking is reinforced by the science of resonance. When our thoughts are in harmony with positive frequencies they are, in a way, amplified and projected into the world around us. Similarly, negative thoughts, like out-of-tune strings, can have a dissonant effect on our inner symphony and the atmosphere we inhabit.

The conscious choice to tune our thoughts, aligning them

with frequencies of love, joy and positivity, is akin to tuning an instrument for a grand performance. It is an act of self-care and a gift to the world around us. In this intricate piece of frequencies, where each thought contributes to the cosmic symphony, we discover the immense influence we have on the tone of our own lives and those of others. Just as a careful musicians tune their instrument before a performance, let us tune our thoughts to the highest vibrations of love and compassion. For in this harmonious tuning, we find not only inner peace and joy but also contribute to the beautiful melody of collective consciousness.

In 1991, Dr. J. Andrew Armour, a prominent cardiologist, discovered that the heart is not just a muscle pumping blood but also contains a complex nervous system with around 40,000 neurons. This network, aptly called the "little brain" by Dr. Armour, resides in the heart and allows the organ to function independently of the brain and make decisions.

This discovery opens a fascinating perspective on the interaction between the heart and the brain and how both organs are involved in regulating our physiological and emotional well-being. The "little brain" in the heart not only has the ability to process information but also to learn and remember. It can quickly respond to changes in the body and environment, making it an integral part of our ability to survive and thrive.

Just as our thoughts and emotions create resonances that impact our mental state, the signals and impulses generated by the "little brain" in the heart can resonate throughout our body. This phenomenon highlights the close connection between our physical and emotional health, where both the brain and the heart play a role in establishing a harmonious balance that can have a profound effect on our overall well-being. It illustrates the complexity of the inner symphony that shapes our humanity: thoughts, emotions, and physiology work together harmoniously.

The discovery of the "little brain" in the heart offers an interesting perspective on my role as a musician. In the context of a concert and my interaction with music, this discovery suggests that playing with the heart is just as valuable, if not more so, than relying solely on the brain.

Playing with my heart allows me to delve into a deeper layer of expression and connection. The "little brain" in the heart has the ability to understand and convey emotions, and this capability can infuse the music I produce. It enables me to intuitively navigate the emotional resonances of the music, creating a deeper connection with both the music and the audience.

Rather than strictly relying on the analytical powers of the brain, which are important but can sometimes limit spontaneity and emotional depth, playing with the heart offers a more fluid and organic approach. It allows me to feel and communicate the emotional nuances in each note, making my music more vibrant and captivating. In this approach, I can find a unique way to reach the audience and leave a lasting impression.

The electric field of the heart is 40 to 60 times stronger than that of the brain, offering a fascinating insight into the heart's role as a center of consciousness and resonance. While playing, my musical expression is not only conveyed through the vibrations of the strings but also through the subtle resonances of my heart. The heart, as the seat of emotion and intuition, emits energy waves that go beyond physical presence, creating an invisible connection with the audience.

Even more impressive is the electromagnetic field of the heart, which is 5000 times stronger than that of the brain. The comparison with the power of musical resonance during a concert is remarkable. The magnetic field of the heart not only surrounds the body but also extends into the surrounding space. Similarly, the music flowing from my instrument seems not confined to the concert hall; it spreads like an ethereal wave, enveloping the listeners in an enchanting sound experience.

In this context, the heart is not only seen as a physical organ pumping blood but as a source of energetic frequencies permeating the fabric of our experience. When I am on stage and my fingers touch the strings, a play of resonances occurs: those of the strings, the body of the instrument, and the pulsing electromagnetic field of my heart. This interplay creates a unique sound world that is not only heard but also felt, forming a deep connection between my heartbeat and the pulses of the music.

It is a dance of energies: the heart takes the lead and guides the notes on a journey through space and time. The science behind the power of the heart opens the door to a holistic understanding of musical expression, where it is not only about skill and emotion but also about the subtle resonances of the heart that enrich and deepen the musical experience. Thus, each concert becomes not just an auditory odyssey but also a comforting journey through the power of resonance and the interaction between music and heartbeat.

CHAPTER 6

SCIENCE, SPIRITUALITY, AND MUSIC IN HARMONY

*D*riven more by experience than by pure belief, I inherited the curious nature of my father, who dedicated his life to medical research. Spirituality has been a constant companion throughout my life, but I have always quickly brought my wandering steps back to earth. My approach has been to directly integrate spiritual teachings into the here and now, to experience them in practice, and to observe what results manifest.

In the rich world of music, an enchanting connection unfolds, inspired by an intriguing statement often attributed to Pythagoras: "Music can be used as medicine." This profound statement has a transformative effect on my own journey of discovery, where my curious investigative mind merges perfectly with the passionate musician within me.

Pythagoras, considered by some as the "Father of Music," not only laid the foundations of geometry and mathematics but also discovered the essence of musical intervals. His teachings encompassed the healing potential of sound and harmonic frequencies, pioneering the idea of prescribing music as a form of medicine. This vision profoundly altered my perspective on music and motivated me to dedicate a significant part of my life to uncovering the deeper meanings and effects that my music induces in people, especially during my live performances. I will elaborate on this in the upcoming chapters.

In light of faith and the evolution of scientific knowledge, I reflect on a surprising historical fact. In the past, many believed that only wooden boats could float, while metal boats were thought to sink. This belief was deeply ingrained and seemed logical, based on superficial observations.

However, as is often the case, scientific research and understanding eventually proved otherwise. The discovery and formulation of the laws of buoyancy, such as Archimedes' principle, showed that the material itself was not the sole determinant of buoyancy. It is not just about the type of material but also about the displacement of water, which creates an upward force that determines buoyancy.

This historical example interestingly illustrates how our beliefs and perceptions can be questioned and altered by scientific discoveries. What was once considered indisputable has later been supplemented by a deeper understanding and more precise information. This reminds us that faith, like science, can continually evolve as we learn more about the world around us.

Instead of blindly adhering to abstract concepts, I have sought ways to make spirituality tangible and relevant in my daily reality. Driven by a curious mind, this approach led me to actively engage in spiritual practices and philosophies. I believe that spirituality is not merely a theoretical concept but something to be lived and embodied to grasp its true depth.

My father's devotion to medicine also influenced me to adopt a pragmatic approach. I am interested in understanding the practical applications of spiritual principles and how they can enrich our daily lives. It is an ongoing journey, a school of learning in the present moment, where I am open to the experiences that unfold and ready to reap the fruits of my efforts. This approach has enriched my spiritual journey and helped me understand and embody the value of spirituality in my own life path.

The integration of science, particularly in the context of quantum physics, has added depth to my understanding of my spiritual journey. The fascinating and sometimes mysterious behavior of subatomic particles has enriched my understanding of the underlying interconnectedness of everything in the universe. The idea that everything is interconnected, as suggested by quantum physics, reflects the core of my spiritual beliefs.

In my artistic expressions, whether in music or sculpture, I have consciously incorporated these scientific insights. My music and visual art are imbued with an awareness of an underlying energy, a fabric that permeates everything. Just as quantum particles exhibit seemingly unpredictable behavior, I strive to create space for spontaneity and surprise in my creations.

The connection between science and spirituality has enriched my art with layers of deeper meaning. The idea that the act of creation itself resonates with the fundamental elements of the universe adds another dimension to my artistic expression. It is an ongoing journey of discovery: I explore and seek to understand both the mysteries of the universe and the inner journey of the soul.

Essentially, my spiritual journey, influenced by scientific knowledge, manifests in my art as a synergy of wonder at the mystery of existence and a conscious invitation to explore it. It is a continuous process of learning, experimentation, and evolution, where I use both my scientific and spiritual compass to navigate my unique artistic path.

In the rich symphony of my artistic exploration, the chapter "Information-Inspiration" is presented as an enchanting melody. In this, the essence of my curiosity resonates.

In these two words, I reveal the subtle interplay between form and spirit, hidden within the linguistic richness of many languages. In "information" lies the form, and in "inspiration" lies the spirit. The goal of my life has always been to cherish the alchemical transformation from form to spirit. By consciously engaging in this process, the harvest from both worlds becomes apparent to me.

The sequence of this journey is crucial. First, I direct my quest towards form, the tangible expression of ideas. Then, transformation occurs in the spiritual dimension, where magic transcends the constraints of time and space. It is here, in this transcendental sphere, that the magnificent result emerges, a blooming of emotions deeply intertwined with my musical performances.

When I dive into books in search of information, a magical transformation takes place. The information I gather not only serves as a source of knowledge but also opens the door to infinite inspiration for my artistic creations.

In this fascinating journey of learning and creation, the philosophy of Rudolf Steiner emerges, in which the aspect of forgetting plays an intriguing role. Steiner suggests that we must first learn, then forget what we have learned, and finally, on a deeper level, truly understand. It is a cyclical process of absorption, letting go, and integration, where forgetting is not seen as a deficiency but rather as a necessary step in the evolution of understanding and wisdom. Just as form transforms into spirit, our knowledge also evolves through the cycle of learning and forgetting.

He emphasized the idea that learning is not merely about acquiring new knowledge but also about having the ability to let go of certain information and make room for further development and understanding. However, Steiner's views are rooted in his esoteric philosophy, and not all aspects of his thought are accepted universally in the academic world or educational institutions. It is a perspective specifically tied to anthroposophy, and opinions on it may vary.

In my quest to understand the learning process, I have discovered valuable perspectives that have enriched my creative freedom. The realization, inspired by Rudolf Steiner's ideas, that learning is not simply a one-way path of acquiring new knowledge but rather a cyclical process of learning, forgetting, and relearning, has opened doors to a deeper understanding. The ability to consciously let go of information has proven essential to my artistic development, allowing me to create space for new perspectives and creative impulses. This alchemy between form and spirit, guided by the understanding of forgetting as an integral part of learning, has enriched my artistic journey and enabled me to experience deeper emotional resonances in my musical performances.

The process of digesting an apple offers a fascinating analogy for understanding the creative cycle in music. When we consume an apple, it undergoes a complex process of decomposition and assimilation in our digestive system. The fibers, sugars, and nutrients are gradually broken down and absorbed by our bodies. Curiously, the inherent energy of the apple is only fully released when it is completely digested.

This parallel with music reflects the idea that the notes on a score, as given entities, do not yet contain the full potential of musical energy. After the "digestion" of the notes by the musician—interpreting them, feeling them, and blending them with their own expression—the true power of musical emotion emerges. Forgetting thus serves as a crucial link in this creative process, where the original form of the notes is transcended and converted into musical emotion. Just as the energy of the apple is released only after complete digestion, the true magic of music comes to life when information is forgotten and inspiration can flourish.

In my musical learning process, I discovered that simply

reading and playing the notes is only the first step. Reading the notes, no matter how perfectly executed, does not automatically convey the magic to the audience. Musical notes become vibrant music when they are "digested" through my understanding and interpretation. It is the process of internal assimilation and comprehension that ignites the spark of emotion, and only then can I share a sincere and profound musical story with my listeners. It's not just about perfection in playing but about the deeper meaning that emerges when I fully understand and integrate the notes.

I see a parallel with the principle of physics that energy cannot be created or destroyed but can only change forms. The energy in the atoms of an apple is already present and is released during the digestion process. Similarly, the emotional energy in musical notes is intrinsically present and comes to life when it is understood and interpreted.

In both quantum physics and my approach to music, the essence of energy is recognized as constant, though in different forms. In my "musical digestive process," I see myself as a channel transforming the inherent emotional energy of musical notes and transmitting it into an experience that the audience can feel. It is a continuous cycle of understanding, interpretation, and transformation, where musical energy changes form but never disappears.

Examining the general properties of atoms, the largest part of an atom consists of empty space, and the mass of subatomic particles (like protons and neutrons) is a fraction of the total mass-energy of the atom, as formulated in Einstein's famous equation $E=mc2E=mc^2E=mc2$. This equation captures the relationship between energy (E), mass (m), and the speed of light (c). In the context of the mass-energy relationship, the ratio between matter and energy is essential for understanding the fundamental nature of matter at the quantum scale.

In this fascinating duality, we observe that this empty space is not truly empty; instead, it is filled with energy. At the infinitesimally small scale, atoms are predominantly characterized by the presence of energy, with matter forming only a fraction.

This scientific discovery sheds unique light on the nature of matter and energy. In my musical exploration, a similar phenomenon is reflected. Each musical note, however minimal its material appearance, carries within itself an abundance of emotional energy manifested in sound and melody.

The relationship between matter and empty space in atoms, akin to the relationship between musical notes and the emotional power they radiate, is truly remarkable. As a musician and artist, I constantly strive to understand and capture this energetic essence in my music, allowing the audience to share in the depth of this creative journey. It is an ongoing quest for harmony between science and art, where the quantum principles of matter and energy serve as a metaphor for the subtle dynamics between music and emotion.

In other words, it seems that it's not so much the notes I play that matter, but rather the way I play them. The specific tones I choose constitute only a fraction of the information needed to evoke emotion in the audience. It's not just about the composition of the notes but rather about how I interpret them, the nuances I introduce, and the depth of my interpretation.

In many ways, this principle is similar to the heart of quantum physics, where the intrinsic nature of a particle is not solely determined by its specific properties but also by its behavior and interactions at the subatomic level. Just as in music, where the expression and interpretation of notes are crucial to their impact on the audience, it seems that our manner of acting and communicating is as important as the specific characteristics of what we do.

Our brain, a complex and fascinating organ, is composed of two hemispheres, each with its unique functions and characteristics. The left hemisphere is often associated with logic, analysis, and language skills. It is the part that helps us solve problems, understand structures, and perform sequential tasks. This half seems to thrive in order and rationality.

On the other hand, we have the right hemisphere, often considered the creative brain. This part of our brain is involved in pattern recognition, art appreciation, understanding emotions, and processing information in a more holistic way. It appears to thrive on intuition and imagination, playing a crucial role in making connections between different concepts.

Interestingly, although these two halves seem to have different specialties, they constantly collaborate. It's not so much a matter of "either/or" but rather "both at once." Our ability to reason logically and think creatively, to analyze and feel, stems from the harmonious interaction between these two brain hemispheres.

In a perfect symphony, each section of the orchestra has its own role, but the ultimate masterpiece is created through their collaboration. The same goes for our brain; both halves contribute to the beautiful complexity of our capacity for thought and complement each other to enable a fuller understanding and experience of the world around us.

When approaching the metaphorical score of life, it seems there are different ways to play the notes. Compare this to a musical composition where the two hemispheres of the brain play important roles, each with its own style and approach.

On one side, we have the rational precision of the left hemisphere, which, like an experienced conductor, reads and interprets the notes on paper with accuracy. This is the part that thinks analytically, recognizes structures, and follows the logical line. In the playing of mental notes, the left hemisphere enjoys directing, unraveling the complex score, and shaping the melody with a keen eye for detail.

On the other hand, we have the improvisational freedom of the right hemisphere, which, like an enthusiastic soloist, brings the notes to life through singing and dancing. Here, the music of the moment is felt rather than read. Intuition and creativity guide the melody, and the notes seem to flow effortlessly.

Ultimately, notes played with the right hemisphere often carry a deeper sound and meaning. It's as if the interpretation, the emotional nuance that arises in the moment, adds an extra dimension to the musical experience. This suggests that when we learn to alternate between reading the score with the left hemisphere and improvising with the right hemisphere, the harmony and depth of music in our lives are enhanced. It's a dynamic in which both approaches collaborate, resonating the unique melody of our existence in a fuller and richer way.

As the music fills the room, a similar phenomenon seems to occur with the audience. Some listeners take a more intellectual approach, analyzing the notes, unraveling the harmonies, and seeking to understand the deeper structures. In a way, this is the left hemisphere of the audience approaching the music more analytically, like a discerning critic.

On the other hand, we have listeners who fully immerse themselves in the musical experience. They temporarily pause their cognitive brain and allow themselves to be carried away by the emotional waves of the melodies. These listeners seem to embrace the right hemisphere, where intuition and emotion take precedence. They feel the music, live the resonances of the sounds, and let themselves be swept away by the flow of the moment.

The interaction between different listening styles in the audience creates a captivating dynamic. The individual listening experience is enriched, and it also contributes to the collective symphony of emotions floating in the room. Thus, a concert becomes not only a performance of notes but a shared journey where the intellectual and emotional dimensions of the audience come together and reinforce each other.

The deep relationship between emotion and music stretches

through the ages, with roots deeply embedded in our human experience. The Latin word "emotio," meaning "movement," takes on a particular significance in the context of music.

Music has the ability to set emotions in motion, stirring our inner world and taking us on a journey of feelings. A composition can have different movements, and our emotions can also vary and evolve through listening to music.

Immersing ourselves in the sounds of a melody allows us to feel an emotional resonance deeply rooted in our being. Music thus builds a bridge between the present and the past, with the Latin word "emotio" reminding us of the ancestral connection between human movement and the expression of emotion.

In each note, rhythm, and melody, there is a story that touches our emotions and sets them in motion. Music becomes a universal language of emotion, where sounds resonate like words in the listener's heart, and where meaning is not only understood but also felt.

The word "emotion" also holds, with a bit of imagination, a fascinating insight when dissected at its base. It is formed by combining "E" and "motion," literally meaning "energy in motion." This analysis opens the door to a deeper understanding of what emotions truly are: a dynamic flow of energy circulating through our being and manifesting in various states of mind.

Realizing that emotions are "energy in motion," each emotional experience becomes a journey, an inner movement that affects us on a physical, mental, and even spiritual level. This underscores the fact that emotions are not static entities but rather powerful forces flowing through us, driving and coloring our perception of the world around us.

When we apply this view of emotions to music, a captivating connection emerges. Music, as an art of sound and rhythm, has the ability to mobilize and set these inner energies in motion. It becomes a medium through which emotions are not only expressed but also activated, allowing listeners to traverse the spectrum of human feelings.

Thus, when listening to a melody, a symphony, or a single note, we experience not only the sound but also the energy within it. It is the "E" of emotion that moves us, touches us, and connects us to the deeper layers of our human existence. Music is not only heard but also felt, as a vibrant expression of the energy inherent in our emotions.

In the interplay of emotions and well-being, the delicate balance of homeostasis reveals itself. This complex dance between internal processes and psychological experiences offers insight into our emotional state intertwined with our bodily well-being.

Emotions, deep resonances of our inner landscape, surpass mere mental experiences. They weave through the fibers of our physiological tissues and subtly influence hormonal balances. Joy, sadness, fear, or anger are not just abstractions; they express themselves in the language of cortisol and endorphins.

The immune system, the guardian of health, is under the influence of this emotional symphony. Prolonged stress, a dissonant note in this harmonious piece, can weaken the immune system, while positive emotions strengthen it. The heart, sharing its rhythm with our feelings, dances to the tunes of joy or is weighed down by the burden of persistent stress.

At the microscopic level, neurotransmitters such as serotonin and dopamine regulate emotional melodies. These chemical messengers, permeating the brain, affect not only our mood but also play a role in the internal balance of the nervous system. Imbalances in these neurotransmitters can disrupt well-being.

Even our eating behavior, an apparently everyday act, can interact with emotions. Compulsive eating, for example as a result of stress, can disturb the harmony of our nutritional intake, thereby generating metabolic imbalance.

In summary, in the symphony of human existence, emotion plays a central role in maintaining or disrupting homeostasis. A healthy emotional state becomes an ally of the body in maintaining balance, while prolonged negative emotions, like dissonant chords, can disrupt the fragile equilibrium. Understanding and cultivating our emotional well-being thus becomes a crucial note in the melody of holistic health.

The influence of music on the nervous system is a fascinating aspect of the relationship with the human body. Music can not only affect emotions but also have a profound effect on the balance between the sympathetic and parasympathetic nervous systems, also known as the accelerator and brake of our body.

The world is often driven by acceleration, corresponding to the sympathetic nervous system, which is associated with the "fight or flight" response and is activated during stressful situations. Unfortunately, many of us are caught in the constant rat race of daily life.

Herein lies the role of music. Studies suggest that listening to soothing music, particularly with gentle and calming tones, can slow down the sympathetic nervous system and activate the parasympathetic nervous system. The parasympathetic nervous system, known as the "rest and digest" system, is responsible for calming the body after stressful situations.

Positive thoughts, such as those evoked by listening to emotionally rich music, have an intriguing biochemical effect. Stress hormones, such as cortisol, show a decrease, leading to normalization of blood sugar levels and reduced blood pressure. This indicates a profound therapeutic potential of music, not only for emotional well-being but also for the physiological health of the body. It is a fascinating area where art, science, and well-being converge.

Deep within my beliefs resonates a powerful melody: the certainty that music can directly contribute to our health. This conviction is rooted in the rich harmonies of my life's journey, where the nyckelharpa serves as a guide, and where its sounds reach not only the ears but also the essence of our well-being.

As an inspired traveler on the path of music and health, I have experienced how the vibrations of sounds resonate with the subtle rhythms of the body. The melodies, woven with care and passion, seem to engage in a direct dialogue with the cells, neurotransmitters, and hormones that orchestrate our inner symphony.

In my art, an alchemical play of sound and emotion unfolds, revealing a profound belief that music is more than just a pleasant sound. It is a powerful ally in the quest for balance, a source of healing.

By touching the strings of the nyckelharpa, I not only feel the vibrations of the notes but also the resonance with the listener. Each tone thus becomes a gentle caress, an invitation to balance, a reminder of the intrinsic connection between music and well-being.

The research of Dr. John Stuart Reid, with his revolutionary blood experiments and the use of the CymaScope instrument, has also profoundly impacted my perception of music and is a crucial component of my book. Dr. Reid, a prominent pioneer in the field of acoustic science, has created a fascinating link between sound and human physiology through his intriguing blood experiments. By exposing blood to various musical tones, he demonstrated that sound waves can elicit direct responses in the blood, highlighting the healing potential of music.

The CymaScope instrument, developed by Dr. Reid, has provided unprecedented insights into the visual manifestations of sound vibrations. This instrument allows us to visualize sound in a unique way, enabling observation of the complex patterns of vibrational frequencies. The combination of Dr. Reid's blood experiments and the use of the CymaScope has further deepened my understanding of the profound relationship between sound and human biology.

In this chapter, I have delved deeper into these intriguing discoveries and explored the power of understanding and harnessing the healing benefits of music in contemporary society. The work of Dr. John Stuart Reid serves as a guiding source of inspiration, and I believe his innovative approaches provide us with a better understanding of the transformative potential of sound and music in the realm of human health and well-being.

In this symphony of beliefs and experiences, I am convinced that music is not a luxury but rather an essential component of a healthy life. It is a universal language that speaks not only to our ears but also penetrates deeply into the core of who we are. Music is not incidental; it is a source of vitality, a companion on the path to well-being.

In concluding this chapter, my deep belief is that the sounds we create nourish the soul and also promote the health of the body. In the cadence of this melody, we find an enduring truth: music is not merely an art form but a vital force that invites us to dance to the rhythms of well-being.

CHAPTER 7

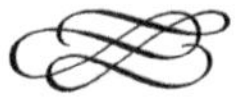

HEALING HARMONY

My exploration of the effect of music on the listener took an unexpected turn when I delved into the processes of healing. Although I never aspired to become a music therapist myself, my research into the healing power of music evolved into an exciting journey. This exploration began with the discovery of Nikola Tesla's ideas, which proved to be a captivating starting point for understanding the influence of sound and vibrations on our well-being.

What if the impact of music extended to the core of our physical being, where vibrations and tones are not just audible but also palpable? Can music create a deep and healing resonance that brings our body and mind to a state of balance and harmony?

Our body, striving for homeostasis, seeks balance and stability. Can music serve as a guide on this journey towards inner equilibrium? Can certain sounds and rhythms direct the homeostatic dance within our bodies, not only alleviating symptoms but perhaps also initiating healing processes?

This exploration goes beyond the soothing effect of a gentle melody. What if music could not only influence our mood but also contribute to the healing of ailments? Different tones carry different frequencies and resonances. From deep bass notes to the sparkling heights of string instruments, each tone has the potential to influence specific aspects of our physiology. In this journey of discovery, we will understand how different sounds serve as keys to various forms of healing.

Nikola Tesla, a visionary inventor and pioneer in electricity and energy, was known for frequently discussing the importance of frequencies in understanding the secrets of the universe. He is attributed with the phrase: "If you want to understand the secrets of the universe, think in terms of energy, frequency, and vibration."

Tesla believed that everything in the universe exists in the form of energy vibrating at different frequencies. According to him, the keys to understanding and mastering the natural world could be found by comprehending and manipulating these energetic waves. He experimented with different forms of energy transmission and resonance, laying the groundwork for many modern technological applications.

In light of Tesla's philosophy, it is fascinating to consider music as a manifestation of these universal principles. Music, composed of a series of sound waves with specific frequencies, can be seen as a form of art that speaks directly to the essence of the universe's vibratory nature. The idea that frequencies play a role not only in technological advancements but also in art forms like music opens the door to a deeper understanding of the connection between human experience and the cosmic fabric of energy.

My journey into the influence of sound and vibrations on our well-being led me to fascinating experiments, including Chladni's plates. Here, I encountered an engaging professor who linked sound frequencies to their visible effects. In this experiment, it became evident that higher frequencies created more complex patterns on the Chladni plate. These visual manifestations brought me closer to understanding the power of frequencies and their ability to shape our physical reality.

Ernst Chladni was a German physicist and music theorist who lived from 1756 to 1827. He is particularly known for his contributions to the study of sound and vibrations. Chladni conducted experiments with vibrating plates, leading to the development of what is now known as Chladni patterns. These patterns illustrate how sound waves affect physical objects, such as a metal plate covered with powder.

His work influenced various fields, including acoustics and the study of vibrations. The Chladni plate experiment, which made vibrations visible by moving powder on a vibrating plate, was one of his important contributions. Chladni's experiments provided valuable insights into the relationship between sound and matter, contributing to the development of acoustics and the study of vibrations.

The Chladni plate experiment offers a fascinating method for visually observing the interaction between sound frequencies and matter. In this experiment, a metal plate is positioned horizontally on a frame, and a fine powder, such as sand or talcum powder, is spread across it. The plate is then vibrated either by rubbing along its edge or by applying sound waves from below.

The vibrations cause the powder to move to areas where the plate does not vibrate, known as nodes. Simultaneously, the areas where the vibration is most intense remain free of powder, creating complex patterns. By varying the frequency, researchers can produce different patterns on the plate. Higher frequencies typically result in more detailed and intricate patterns.

The experiment provides a visual demonstration of how sound frequencies can directly influence the physical structure of matter. Research on these patterns at various frequencies contributes to the understanding of resonance and vibrations in relation to sound.

Higher frequencies tend to produce more complex and beautiful structures. This reminds me of our music industry, which over the years has increasingly eliminated so-called "inaudible" frequencies to save memory when storing music. As a result, the most beautiful frequency structures, as demonstrated by the Chladni experiment, have disappeared. This raises the question: are these frequencies necessary? Are we missing out on the full spectrum of music due to this, and is there something that we could be feeling but not perceiving with our auditory organs?

When music is digitally compressed, frequencies outside the range of human hearing are often omitted. Although these frequencies are not directly audible, they may contribute to the overall experience and resonance of the music. The Chladni experiment shows that higher frequencies create more complex and visually appealing patterns, suggesting that these frequencies play an essential role in the richness and depth of the musical experience. If these subtle frequencies are removed, we risk losing part of the emotional and physical impact of the music.

The idea that we not only hear music but also feel it is supported by the experience of live concerts. During a live musical performance, all frequencies are present and can resonate with our bodies in ways that digital recordings cannot replicate. This raises the question of whether live music concerts are the only way to experience music in its entirety.

My journey of discovery, sparked by the fascination with the Chladni plate experiment, led me to an exciting new phase: the work of Masaru Emoto. His research on the influence of music on water crystals has paved the way for a deeper understanding of how sound frequencies can have a direct impact on the structure of matter.

Masaru Emoto was a Japanese researcher renowned for his work on water crystals. His research focused on the influence of words, music, and intention on the formation of water crystals. Emoto demonstrated that positive words, thoughts, and music led to the formation of beautiful and symmetrical crystalline structures, while negative influences resulted in distorted and chaotic forms.

His experiments involved exposing water to various stimuli, such as speaking words, playing music, or showing images, and then freezing the water to study the resulting crystals. Emoto gained prominence through his books, such as "Messages from Water" and "The Hidden Messages in Water."

Emoto conducted experiments exposing water to different types of music, claiming that the frequency of vibration and the intention behind the music influenced the formation of water crystals. According to Emoto, playing beautiful music with positive intentions resulted in the formation of exquisite and symmetrical crystals.

In contrast, his research showed that playing harsh music with negative and violent lyrics led to the formation of distorted and chaotic water crystals. Thus, the vibrations and emotional content of music influence the structure of water.

The difference between the crystals formed by positive and negative music, according to Emoto, highlighted the potential impact of music on water and, by extension, on the environment.

Our bodies are largely composed of water, which plays a crucial role in understanding the impact of sound frequencies on our health. Depending on factors such as age, sex, and body composition, the percentage of water in an adult body is generally around 60%.

Water is not only a fundamental element for our survival; it also acts as a medium sensitive to the vibrations and frequencies it is exposed to. This phenomenon becomes even more astonishing when we consider that sound waves can indeed propagate through water. Consequently, the sound frequencies we are exposed to provoke various reactions at the cellular level.

When considering the essence of music as a fusion of vibrations, energy, and frequencies, and recognizing their direct influence on water, a substance abundant in our bodies, a reflection arises. Is it not reasonable to say that music, in turn, has a direct impact on our physical constitution? The interaction of these elements forms a subtle yet potentially powerful link between music and the human body, where the resonances of tones traverse the liquid structures of our body.

In the seemingly boundless landscape of scientific research, the healing power of music has captivated the attention of curious minds. Countless studies have been devoted to unraveling the intriguing link between music and healing, and their findings reveal a captivating spectrum of possibilities.

THE NEUROLOGICAL BALLET OF MELODIES

In-depth research into the neurological effects of music has demonstrated how melodies perform a true ballet in our brains. Studies show that music not only activates emotions but also influences neurotransmitter production, triggering a cascade of responses that enhance well-being.

STRESS RELIEF AND THE CORTISOL DUET

An impressive number of studies have explored the impact of music on stress levels. One notable example reveals how listening to certain genres of music can lead to a reduction in the stress hormone, cortisol. These findings pave the way for using music as a powerful tool to relieve stress and promote emotional well-being.

Music has held a special place in our lives since time immemorial. Whether marking significant milestones, expressing emotions, or creating ambiance, the power of music is undeniable. One of the most fascinating aspects of music is its ability to foster relaxation, which has both direct and indirect benefits for our health. Music can help reduce stress and strengthen our immune system.

When we listen to music that we find enjoyable, our bodies respond in various ways. Our breathing may become calmer, our heart rate may slow down, and we may experience a sense of calm and well-being. These physical responses are signs that our bodies are relaxing. A crucial aspect of this relaxation is the reduction of the stress hormone, cortisol. Cortisol is produced by the adrenal glands and plays a significant role in our "fight or flight" response to stress. While cortisol is helpful in acute stress situations, chronic stress can lead to consistently elevated levels of cortisol, which can be harmful to our health. Prolonged exposure to high cortisol levels can suppress the immune system, lead to high blood pressure, weight gain, and other health issues.

THE HARMONY OF HEART RATE AND RHYTHM

Research on the effect of rhythmic patterns and heartbeats on our bodies has yielded interesting results. Studies indicate that certain rhythms can synchronize with our heart rate, producing not only a calming effect but potentially benefiting cardiovascular health as well. This is a fascinating exploration of the harmony between music and the rhythms of our physical being.

THE TONES OF PAIN RELIEF

In the context of pain management, researchers have also examined the role of music. Examples illustrate how music therapy can be effective in reducing the perception of pain, particularly in patients recovering from surgery or suffering from chronic pain.

Let's delve deeper into these fascinating studies and understand how music awakens our emotions and also plays an intrinsic role in promoting our physical and mental well-being.

In the vast expanse of musical exploration and medical breakthroughs, the Tomatis method provides unique insights into the intriguing link between music and auditory problems. Dr. Alfred A. Tomatis, a French physician and pioneer in audiology, developed this innovative approach to treat auditory issues by specifically harnessing the harmonies of Mozart's music.

According to Dr. Tomatis, our ears do not merely function as sound receptors; they also play a vital role in our overall well-being. He believed that targeted stimulation of the ears could not only help improve auditory issues but also influence other aspects of the human experience.

At the heart of the Tomatis method is the use of Wolfgang Amadeus Mozart's harmonious compositions. According to Tomatis, the complex structures and rhythms in Mozart's music have a stimulating effect on the auditory cortex, shaping and strengthening it. Mozart was considered a healer of the auditory system.

In addition to addressing hearing problems, Dr. Tomatis suggested that his method also had beneficial effects on emotional well-being. Improved hearing would trigger a chain reaction of positive effects, such as increased energy, enhanced concentration, and emotional balance.

The Tomatis method impressively illustrates the therapeutic potential of music. The idea that the refined sounds of Mozart's compositions not only provide aesthetic pleasure but also act as a therapeutic tool for restoring hearing opens the door to a deeper understanding of how music can influence our physical and emotional well-being.

Besides Dr. Tomatis, there are other instances where renowned composers and their music have been used as a form of therapy. A notable example is the use of Johann Sebastian Bach's music in music therapy.

Bach's music is known for its complexity and depth, and some researchers and therapists believe that listening to his compositions can contribute to emotional healing and stress reduction. The mathematical precision and harmonic structures of Bach's works have a calming effect and are often used to alleviate anxiety and tension.

In the broader context of music therapy, different genres and composers are used depending on the specific needs of the patient. Music therapists tailor their choices based on the emotional, psychological, and physical goals of the therapy. This can range from classical music to contemporary styles, depending on what is considered most beneficial for the individual patient.

While there is scientific research on the effects of music therapy, it is important to note that the application of specific composers as a healing method often depends on the subjectivity of the patient and the therapist.

There are other examples of using music and specific composers in the context of healing, such as the work of Dr. Fred Schwartz. This American physician used Johann Sebastian Bach's music in the treatment of psychiatric patients. He believed in the healing power of this composer's music and incorporated it into his therapeutic approach. He viewed the rhythm and structure of Bach's compositions as stimulating for the brain and conducive to emotional stability.

This example highlights the fact that different composers can have specific effects on individuals. Each therapist selects the most appropriate music, based on the patient's needs and responses.

Another example of using specific composers in music therapy is the work of Dr. Oliver Sacks, a renowned neurologist and writer. Dr. Sacks describes cases in his book *Musicophilia* where he observed the healing power of music.

In a particular case, Dr. Sacks describes the effect of Wolfgang Amadeus Mozart's music on a patient with Parkinson's disease. The patient, who had difficulties walking and moving, showed a significant improvement in motor abilities while listening to Mozart's music. Dr. Sacks noted that the rhythmic and melodic structures of Mozart's music positively influenced the patient's neurological patterns.

It is interesting to see how the lives of composers are often intertwined with the music they create, and Johann Sebastian Bach's *6 Sonatas and Partitas* add a profound emotional aspect to this. When Bach composed these six sonatas and partitas for solo violin, he was in mourning after the death of his beloved wife, Maria Barbara Bach.

It is worth noting that the manuscript bears the words "Sei solo a violino senza basso accompagnato." There might be more to this than just a musical instruction. In Italian, "Sei solo" could be interpreted as "you are alone." Bach, known for his meticulous approach and attention to detail, surely did not choose his words lightly.

One interpretation could be that Bach, in his profound solitude and grief after the loss of his wife, addresses the violin as a companion in his solitary journey. By saying "Sei solo"—"You are alone"—he might be expressing that the violinist, in playing these challenging pieces, can experience the loneliness that Bach himself felt.

The power of music to convey emotions, both for the composer and the performer, is once again strongly evident here. The notes are not merely an artistic expression but also a bridge between the deepest feelings of the composer and the interpreter of his music. The fact that Bach wove his personal emotions into the music makes these masterpieces even more impressive and timeless.

The uniqueness in the example of Bach's *6 Sonatas and Partitas* is not necessarily a direct form of medical music therapy but rather an indirect emotional therapy. Bach used his musical creativity as an outlet to process his deep grief and loneliness following the death of his wife, Maria Barbara Bach.

Instead of seeking external help, as one might do today with modern music therapy, Bach chose to express his feelings directly through his compositions. The violin, as a solo instrument without accompaniment, seems to engage in a dialogue with the composer himself. By writing this music, Bach created a space for introspection and catharsis, allowing him to explore and address his own emotional state.

This beautifully illustrates the healing power of music on a more personal level. Music can serve as a form of self-expression and self-therapy, where the composer or performer understands themselves on a deeper level and channels their emotions. Thus, the creation and performance of music can become a therapeutic process, even if that was not the explicit goal.

Very concretely, there is also the example of kidney stones. Hard deposits forming in the kidneys can be broken down using sound waves in a medical procedure called extracorporeal shock wave lithotripsy (ESWL). During this non-invasive treatment, powerful sound waves are used to pulverize kidney stones, making them small enough to be naturally expelled from the body.

The procedure begins by directing shock waves precisely at the location of the kidney stone. These shock waves, generated by an external device, penetrate the body and break the kidney stone into smaller fragments. The process uses the properties of sound waves to apply targeted force, crushing the stones without requiring cuts or incisions. Although this medical process specifically targets kidney stones, it illustrates the use of sound waves to treat certain medical conditions by applying energy precisely to a specific area.

In my quest for a deeper understanding of music and its healing power, I cannot ignore the influence of Pythagoras. This ancient Greek mathematician and philosopher transformed my understanding of music through his discoveries in the realms of sound, vibration, and numbers. Like Pythagoras, I have let my curiosity be guided by the connections between sound and mathematics.

Pythagoras was indeed interested in the relationship between sound, vibrations, and numbers. He is often credited with discovering certain principles of harmony and music related to numerical ratios. One of his most well-known contributions is the discovery of the so-called Pythagorean tuning, a method of tuning musical instruments based on simple ratios of whole numbers. Pythagoras experimented with strings on a monochord, a simple musical instrument with a single string, and found that the ratios of the lengths of the strings produced certain harmonious intervals when plucked.

Pythagoras' discovery illustrates how understanding frequencies and vibration ratios, derived from his mathematical knowledge, impacted the development of music theory. His work laid the foundation for later music theorists and contributed to the understanding of harmony in music. Pythagoras also believed in the cosmic significance of harmony and music. He considered the movements of celestial bodies as harmonic movements and asserted that the universe was constructed according to mathematical principles. This philosophy contributed to the notion of music as a fundamental and universal principle deeply connected to the structure of the universe.

One of the most intriguing anecdotes illustrating his approach is the story of the blacksmith. According to tradition, Pythagoras passed by a blacksmith's shop and heard the sound of hammer blows. He observed with interest that the sounds emanating from the blacksmith's shop were harmonizing with each other. Upon investigating, he discovered that the hammers used to shape the metal had varied weights.

Out of curiosity, Pythagoras decided to weigh the hammers and found that the ratios of their weights were simple whole numbers. For example, if one hammer weighed half as much as another, they produced a harmonious sound when used together. This discovery led to Pythagoras' idea that simple ratios produced harmonic sound.

The episode of the blacksmith highlights not only Pythagoras' keen observational skills but also his ability to apply principles of harmony to everyday situations. It underscores how he studied the world around him and discovered essential principles of music in seemingly simple events. This story emphasizes Pythagoras' ingenious thinking and how his ideas have shaped our understanding of music and harmony.

Pythagoras' connection between vibrations and the universe extended beyond musical harmonies. He believed that numbers and ratios formed the foundation of the cosmos. In his famous theorem, initially focused on musical harmony, Pythagoras discovered the relationship between the lengths of strings on a musical instrument and the tones they produced.

These observations led Pythagoras to the concept of the "music of the spheres." He proposed that the movement of celestial bodies such as planets and stars could be understood as a form of celestial music, with the ratios between their orbital periods being harmonic. Pythagoras believed that the universe was imbued with order and harmony, and that these harmonies were reflected through numbers and ratios.

Some of Pythagoras' ideas need to be viewed in a historical context, as not all have been scientifically proven. However, his contribution to the understanding of music, vibrations, and their connection to the universe is invaluable. His philosophical approach paved the way for new discoveries and research in the areas of harmony, numbers, and the relationship between music and the cosmic whole. The mystery of the music of the spheres remains a fascinating field where scientists continue to seek answers to new questions.

Although my understanding of this complex topic is colored by my imagination and curiosity, I recognize that I cannot present peer-reviewed science. My questions are like sparks in the darkness, hoping to ignite a few lights here and there. I hope that the imagination of others may evolve into future science, allowing us to collectively make discoveries that contribute to the well-being of humanity. The mysteries of music, vibrations, and their impact on our bodies are a captivating domain where scientific research and creative imagination can intersect.

In the fabric of creativity and art, one often finds invisible threads mysteriously intertwined by the universe. The following story is an unexpected twist in my own creative journey, a twist that unfolded so perfectly in synchrony that it seemed almost magical.

As I was immersed in writing this book, I experienced the realization of an "authentic" testimonial. Indeed, someone shared with me their healing after having listened my music, thus materializing my ideas. Less than a day later, I received an email that seemed like a gift from the cosmos. A reader, later expressing a desire to attend one of my workshops, shared an emotional experience: my music had been a source of support and comfort during their recovery after a major surgery.

This moment of synchronicity added a new chapter to my own narrative and affirmed the power of art not only to inspire but also to truly heal. It is with great pleasure that I now share this story, highlighting the magic of art and its impact on the lives of others. May this testimonial resonate as an echo of the harmonies we discover together and the connections we share through the universal language of music.

Here unfolds the story of a man who underwent deep neurosurgery in the fall of 2022. He shared his experience of how music can illuminate, support, and console during the darkest moments of life.

Several years ago, scar tissue appeared in my brain, stemming from a distant past, triggering increasing migraines and regular epileptic seizures. The tissue originated from an accident years earlier, unfortunately undetected by the doctors at the local hospital where I was initially treated, who never paid attention to it.

The consensus among neurologists and neurosurgeons was unanimous: removing this scar tissue from this specific location would be an extremely delicate operation. Despite their extensive experience and expertise, the head of neurosurgery even consulted American colleagues. Was it possible to perform this operation without enduring lasting motor or cognitive consequences for the patient?

Three years of extensive research and consultations preceded the actual surgery. I was fully aware of the considerable risks and potential damage looming over those years. The day of admission arrived on September 19, 2022. At the reception, I registered and completed the necessary admission forms. I then proceeded to the neurosurgery department, located high up in the hospital building.

From the tenth floor, my room offered a panoramic view of the city, now seeming distant and inaccessible. After placing my bag on the bed, I took out my portable Bluetooth speaker. A cylindrical device I could hold in my hand, black, waterproof, with a 45-meter range. This device produced powerful sound with deep bass. I had purchased the Bluetooth speaker eight years earlier, and it had proven to be an excellent investment. Not only because of the product itself but also for the music that had accompanied me since then.

Headphones were convenient for personal listening pleasure, but with the Bluetooth speaker, I could arrive somewhere and gently fill the space with music without disturbing others. Subtly, an additional dimension joined the familiar three dimensions characterizing space. A dimension of softness, trust, and comfort. A blissful experience, especially when I regularly rented a cabin in nature. There, I silently and meditatively admired the beauty of nature. But also in the evening at sunset or in the morning at sunrise, sitting behind a large window overlooking the fields, where the music of Stephan Micus, Didier François, Sofie Vanden Eynde, or Michel Bisceglia floated silently in the space yet was still present.

The difference lay in the position you adopted. You could feel in harmony with nature, being a part of it, without the need for music. Millions of years of evolution found their reflection. But you could also be a spectator of this nature, from afar, admiring its beauty and feeling grateful to be allowed to see it. Music helped to reinforce, to perpetuate that feeling; music helped to extend the feeling of gratitude, joy, and euphoria a little longer.

In my hospital room, I placed my Bluetooth speaker on the

windowsill and connected it to my mobile phone. While browsing through my playlists on the streaming service Deezer, mainly of my own composition, I decided to open a playlist with music by Didier François. The soft tones of the music were familiar and partially dispelled the cold, distant atmosphere of the hospital room. The music acted as a companion, supporting me on my journey into the unknown. Faced with complete uncertainty about what to expect, this music felt like a friend by my side. My fate was in the hands of the doctors, and no one could predict with certainty how I would come out of the situation. But music was a familiar constant. It dispelled some of the uncertainty and made me feel more comfortable

The process itself involved several stages. First, the neurosurgeons had to ensure that the area to be removed was indeed the source of the epilepsy. A preparatory procedure, an invasive mapping, was necessary. Electrodes were drilled through the skull from various positions and deeply inserted between the cerebral lobes. These electrodes precisely recorded all brain activity. During this week of mapping, epileptic seizures were triggered, with the electrodes in the brain accurately recording the exact location of the attack.

The preparation for this procedure involved applying a steel frame to the skull. This metal frame was fixed to the skull with screws through the scalp, all of which had to be done while the patient was fully conscious. With the heavy frame on my head, I had to enter the MRI tunnel for imaging. This MRI provided a precise image of the contents of the skull with the steel frame around it, the ultimate spatial reference for the neurosurgeons to guide deep needles through the skull into the brain at the perfect angle, without touching any of the many small blood vessels. Touching a blood vessel would immediately cause a brain hemorrhage. Local anesthesia was applied where the screws were placed in the scalp.

The pain during the application of the steel frame was unbearable. Once the metal device was initially placed on the skull, the various metal components making up the frame had to be aligned to properly encase the head. Using a metal key, the metal bolts holding the components of the frame together were tightened. Every time the doctors touched the metal frame on my head with the metal key, it felt like a large hammer was hitting my skull. The metal on metal transmitted all the vibrations, both mechanical and auditory. The pain was truly unbearable. I screamed in pain, and two nurses had to hold me firmly.

Finally, the frame was secured, followed by the MRI imaging and the transition to the operating room with the assistance of the nurses. A plate with various bright lights shone in my eyes as the doctors and nurses hovered over me. The anesthesiologist repeatedly said, "How are you, sir? Stay relaxed, breathe." Everything was so cold. Everything was so sterile, functional, and rational. Was this the end of life as I had known it up until then? How would I wake up? Fear gripped me, and at that moment, I did not want to proceed with the surgery. But there was no turning back.

I began to cry like a small child, louder and louder. The professor entered the operating room, and I heard the doctors discussing the progress of the preparation and how traumatized the patient was. I felt weaker and weaker, and the light faded.

"Sir? Sir? It's time to wake up." From afar, soft voices reached me, but I did not want to hear them. I ignored the sounds, but the voices remained relentlessly present, almost commanding. "You can wake up now. Just wake up." Vaguely, I saw figures in green uniforms, green caps on their heads. "Are you in pain? Are you in a lot of pain?" I nodded affirmatively. I could not speak. No sound came from my lips. My head was pounding intensely, and my jaws felt crushed. Was it day or night? A nurse passed by regularly, checking the data on the computer screen next to my bed. I was suffering and whispered to her. She turned a valve, and I slid into the void.

Morphine takes effect. I wake up again. All the lights on the ceiling are now shining intensely. There is a lot of activity around me, with people coming and going. A sliding curtain separates me from the rest, and I hear patients groaning to my left and right. A nurse pulls back the plastic curtain and comes to talk to me. They are going to wash me. Two nurses, completely in their routine, seem to wash me from chest to feet. All sense of pride has disappeared. You feel completely at the mercy of the kindness and willingness of others. But these two nurses are kind. They understand that the patient is entirely helpless and experiencing a sense of total loss. They find the right balance between sobriety and gentleness. The professionalism of the nursing staff is evident.

After 24 hours in the post-anesthesia care unit, commonly known as the PACU, I am taken back to my room. The violent migraine persists. Later, the doctors explain that there are different types of headaches. On one hand, there is the dull, throbbing headache throughout the head, resulting from the body's elimination of residual blood. On the other hand, there is the sharp, stabbing headache specific to the side where the skull was opened, caused by the cutting of tissues and nerves inside.

Every few hours, I receive a cocktail of powerful painkillers. I am in a nearly comatose state. I ask the nurse for my phone. Mumbling, I ask her to place my Bluetooth speaker on the nightstand. Extremely tired and confused, I manage to open the playlist with Didier François' music. "Ciaconne," "Toona," "Tilia," and "Promenade d'automne" play very softly, at a minimal volume, from the speaker next to me. The repeat function is activated. I let myself be carried away by the gentle, comforting sounds. Like a warm blanket, the soothing and calming music wraps around me. At that moment, the beautiful exchange of sounds between a human voice and a string instrument acts as an additional painkiller, healing me.

I drift off and wake up, day after day, with this soft music beside me. Almost inaudible to the nurses who come every hour to check my vitals. Didier's music helps me to navigate the unknown and overcome my fear.

Didier's music helps me to endure the intensity of the pain and move forward. The pain from the application of the steel frame lingers for a long time; it is unbearable after the surgery and drains me. The music appears to me as a soothing balm.

The music also helps me to rediscover my humanity. The shame and guilt of my dependence completely disappear. The music comforts me in the temporary loss of my dignity.

Ultimately, the music helps me cherish my gratitude for life and for the nursing staff. I will never forget the kindness of most. Some choose to help others in their weakest and most painful moments.

Music is an essential element in my life. Artists should know that their creations and performances can mean a lot to people. Depending on the situation in which the same piece of music is played, it can serve different roles: inspiring, supporting, comforting, or healing. It costs the artist a lot of energy, time, effort, and sometimes pain to create such beautiful music. I thank Didier and all the others for the beauty they create.

CHAPTER 8

THE HARMONY OF TEMPTATION

Our brains, like a symphonic orchestra of neurons, have their own unique rhythms and patterns. Frequencies, measured in hertz, reflect these inner melodies. Different brain waves, from delta to gamma, represent various states of consciousness, from deep sleep to intense concentration.

Music, a series of structured frequencies, has the power to influence these brain waves. Appropriate tones can synchronize our brains, creating harmony between different parts of our minds. This phenomenon is known as brainwave entrainment, where music acts as the conductor of our inner symphony.

A composer chooses colorful chords; music paints the emotional landscapes of our minds. Frequencies resonate with our emotions on a deep level, capable of enhancing, soothing, or transforming them.

When you listen to music with specific emotional resonance, you realize that it synchronizes your emotions with the frequencies of the melody. This can be a powerful tool for emotional regulation, much like a conductor mastering the dynamics of an orchestra.

This chapter provides only a glimpse into the complex dance

of frequencies within the psyche. As we delve deeper into this sonic sea, we are invited to contemplate the impact of sound on our thoughts, emotions, and ultimately, our well-being.

In the dynamic world of advertising, the art of seduction is a true symphony of strategically placed frequencies. Behind catchy slogans and appealing visuals lies a deeper understanding of how sound frequencies influence consumer psychology.

Advertisers harness the power of auditory recognition. Think of the recognizable tunes that signal our favorite brands are back in the spotlight. These auditory logos, often based on specific frequencies, embed themselves in our memory and automatically evoke associations with a particular product or brand.

The goal of advertising is to provoke emotions. Frequencies are carefully chosen to elicit specific emotional responses. For example, an advertisement for a relaxing spa might use lower frequencies to convey a sense of calm and tranquility, while an ad for an energy drink might opt for higher frequencies to suggest excitement and dynamism.

The rhythm of advertisements follows a pattern designed to capture the viewer's attention. Rapid transitions and catchy rhythms are used to generate energy and excitement, while slower and more consistent cadences can promote a sense of serenity.

In addition to conscious auditory choices, subliminal frequencies also play a role in advertising. Subtle sounds, sometimes even beyond the range of conscious hearing, are strategically used to create a sense of urgency, desire, or curiosity.

As the world of advertising continually evolves, the role of frequencies in the art of seduction deepens. Understanding how sound influences our emotions and decision-making opens the door to a new era of targeted advertising. In this ongoing symphony of frequencies, each advertisement becomes a composition in itself, a masterpiece of seduction awakening our consumer desires.

When the height of billboards was legally restricted, it marked a new era in the advertising world. Advertisers faced the challenge of capturing the public's attention through alternative means. This led to a thorough exploration of the synergy between visuals and sound, aiming to create a powerful sensory experience.

The limitation on physical height encouraged marketers to explore how sound could enhance the impact of visual messages. Rather than relying solely on the grandeur of billboards, they began to harness the power of sound to forge deeper emotional connections with the audience.

This era of sensory advertising brought a wave of creativity. Sound designers and marketers collaborated to find the perfect harmony between auditory and visual elements. The goal was not only to capture attention but also to leave a lasting impression on the consumer's memory.

Frequencies were no longer seen as mere sound waves but as powerful tools to guide emotions. Advertisements began to sound like mini-symphonies, where each note was carefully chosen to evoke a specific response. For instance, a commercial for a refreshing drink might use bright, sparkling sounds to evoke thirst.

The rise of digital advertising provided even more opportunities to integrate sound and visuals. Online platforms enabled interactive ads, engaging consumers in an immersive experience that was both visually and audibly stimulating.

In summary, the restriction on physical height prompted the advertising world to think more deeply about the role of sensory stimuli in message delivery. The quest for perfect harmony between visuals and sound led to a new dimension in advertising, where frequencies act as invisible conductors of the consumer experience.

In the realm of sound design and musical composition, Brian Eno has carved out a unique position as a visionary artist. His masterful ability to weave realms of emotion through sounds and melodies is reflected in a wide range of projects, including the iconic jingle for Microsoft.

As one of the world's largest technology companies, Microsoft sought a sound brand that was not only recognizable but also embodied the company's values and vision. Brian Eno was commissioned for this challenging task, and his contribution profoundly influenced Microsoft's auditory identity.

The jingle, known as the Windows Startup Sound, Is a masterpiece in itself. Eno succeeded in creating a short, simple sound that immediately became associated with the launch of computer systems for users around the world. It became a sonic signature, an announcement of the digital journey awaiting the user.

Eno's impactful work managed to translate abstract concepts like reliability, innovation, and user-friendliness into sound. He captured the essence of Microsoft in tones, making it not only a corporate jingle but also an auditory symbol of a technological era.

Eno's approach to this project demonstrates his deep understanding of the psychology of sound and its power to influence emotions. His work for Microsoft is not just a melody; it's an auditory handshake, a reassuring welcome to the digital world we navigate daily. In the collaboration between Brian Eno and Microsoft, we witness the magic of sound as a powerful tool for bringing brands to life and creating deep connections with their audience.

The iconic Apple startup sound has an interesting history and contributes significantly to the company's brand identity. Jim Reekes, the sound engineer at Apple responsible for creating this sound, played a crucial role in its development.

The sound was initially created for the Macintosh Quadra

computers in 1991. Jim Reekes wanted to craft a recognizable and positive sound that would greet users when powering up their computers. The result was a short, clear, and melodic tone that quickly became associated with the Apple experience.

Steve Jobs, Apple's co-founder, understood the importance of a good user experience, including sounds that could elicit an emotional response. The startup sound became an auditory symbol of the beginning of something new and innovative.

In contrast, Brian Eno takes a different approach in his work for Microsoft. While Apple's startup sound is compact and melodic, Eno is known for his ambient music, including the concept of "generative music," which is designed to constantly change and evolve, contrasting with the static nature of a short startup sound.

However, both approaches illustrate the attention to sound design in the tech world. Apple's startup sound and Brian Eno's ambient compositions both contribute to the user experience on a deeper, almost subconscious level.

Music plays a subtle yet powerful role in the consumer shopping experience, particularly in supermarkets. These stores use carefully selected music to influence the atmosphere, prolong shopping time, and even affect buying behavior.

The tempo, style, and volume of the music in supermarkets are carefully adjusted to achieve the desired effect. Faster tempos can encourage people to move quickly through the aisles, while slower tempos create a relaxing atmosphere, prompting customers to stay longer and potentially buy more. The musical genre can also impact the experience; for example, classical music is sometimes chosen to promote a sense of sophistication and tranquility.

Additionally, the supermarket's target audience is taken into account. Music popular among the store's target demographic can create an emotional connection and enhance the overall shopping experience. The goal is not only to sell products but also to create a pleasant atmosphere that encourages customers to return.

Research has shown that music can influence buying behavior. For instance, the use of calm music can increase wine sales, while faster-tempo music may lead to more impulse purchases. Supermarkets understand the power of music as a silent but effective influencer of consumer behavior, strategically applying this knowledge to optimize the overall shopping experience.

The influence of music on the dining experience in restaurants is extremely varied and heavily depends on the type of restaurant and the desired ambiance. In upscale dining establishments, music is often used as a sophisticated complement to the overall atmosphere. Soft tones, classical music, or jazz are frequently chosen to create a refined environment that matches the quality of the food and service.

In contrast, fast-food or casual dining restaurants often focus on quick consumption and an informal atmosphere. Lively and upbeat music is used to create a positive, energetic ambiance that aligns with the concept of speed and accessibility.

The pace of consumption is also influenced by the choice of music. In upscale dining restaurants, slower music can be used to encourage diners to savor each bite slowly, thus extending the culinary experience. In contrast, fast-food establishments might use faster, more upbeat music to promote customer turnover and create a dynamic environment aligned with the concept of quick consumption.

The power of silence is increasingly recognized, especially in an era where we are constantly exposed to auditory stimuli. Consciously reducing background noise, such as turning off buzzing devices, can have a significant impact on our inner peace and overall well-being.

Many people feel the need for more silence in the evening when the daily hustle and bustle subsides. Turning off sounds like the hum of computers or other electronic devices creates an atmosphere of tranquility. This quietude allows individuals to relax, reduce stress, and create a peaceful environment conducive to calm and reflection.

In Belgium, some stores deliberately choose a soundscape without background music to provide a calm and natural atmosphere for their customers. Avoiding music in this context gives people the opportunity to shop without additional auditory stimuli, allowing them to connect more deeply with the products and the environment.

The trend towards silent spaces and noise-free zones is part of a growing awareness of the impact of sound on our health. It serves as an antidote to the constant barrage of noise we are often exposed to.

The power of silence became strikingly clear during the lockdowns that followed the COVID-19 pandemic. As the world seemed to come to a halt and people were forced into isolation, an unexpected aspect of this period emerged: the beneficial tranquility of silence.

In the absence of the usual noise of daily life, where traffic, crowds, and various activities surround us, a remarkable silence emerged. Streets became quiet, public spaces emptied, and the constant hum of society ceased. This situation offered an opportunity to rediscover the value of silence.

For many, the lockdown became a period of reflection, a chance to escape the noise of the world and focus inward. The lack of external sounds created space for inner silence, allowing people to contemplate, meditate, and connect with their own thoughts and feelings.

The power of this silence proved beneficial for individuals' well-being. It provided an opportunity to reduce stress, calm the mind, and cultivate a sense of inner peace. Many found that the silence during lockdown was an unexpected source of comfort and inspiration.

In the depth of general silence, where only the gentle hum of our brains is audible, a unique form of tranquility manifests. This serene silence goes beyond the absence of external sounds; it is an inner peace that arises from the calm symphony of our own thoughts.

When the world around us becomes quiet, leaving only the faint murmur of the mind, a space for introspection unfolds. The hum of our brains, often imperceptible amidst the clamor of daily life, becomes a companion in the silence. We can listen to the inner melody of our thoughts, a subtle yet constant cadence that fills the silence.

In this calm internal space, a sense of clarity emerges. The noise of the world gives way to a deeper, more authentic silence where we can better understand ourselves. Here, we discover an oasis of tranquility, a refuge where we can escape from constant external stimuli and return to ourselves to find inner peace.

The gentle hum we hear in our thoughts is an intriguing scientific phenomenon. It is attributed to the activity of our brains, which are constantly engaged in processing information, memories, and thoughts. This inner sound, also known as "brain humming" or "mental noise," has various causes and contributes to our understanding of ongoing neurological processes.

This humming results from the electrical activity of neurons in our brain, even at rest. It reflects electrical impulses and communication between neurons. During moments of silence and relaxation, brain networks such as the default mode network (DMN), involved in self-reflection and memory processing, are activated. The humming sound may reflect the coordination of these activities.

Although it is a natural aspect of brain activity, it is not fully understood. Research into the neurological basis of this phenomenon can contribute to a deeper understanding of the complex relationship between mental processes and auditory perception in the context of silence.

The presence of hissing sounds, also known as tinnitus or ringing in the ears, can have a significant impact on a person's well-being. Tinnitus manifests as sounds such as buzzing, ringing, or hissing without an external acoustic source. In conjunction with the humming sound previously discussed in our thoughts, tinnitus illustrates a complex interplay of neurological processes.

For individuals suffering from tinnitus, the constant presence of hissing sounds can become a source of frustration, anxiety, and even stress. The sounds can vary in pitch and intensity, and their origin is often associated with damage to the hair cells in the inner ear. This damage can result from exposure to loud noises, age-related hearing loss, or other underlying medical conditions.

Unlike the brain humming, which is a natural aspect of our neurological activity, tinnitus is a symptom of an underlying problem. It can affect daily functioning, reduce sleep quality, and lead to emotional strain. Research into treatments for tinnitus is ongoing, with approaches ranging from sound management to cognitive-behavioral therapy to reduce its impact.

The association between internal brain humming and tinnitus highlights the complexity of auditory experiences and their consequences on our well-being. Research into these phenomena contributes to a deeper understanding of how sounds, both internal and external, influence our psyche.

R. Murray Schafer, a prominent Canadian composer and acoustic ecologist, is known for his innovative work in the field of sound ecology and acoustics. Schafer has made significant contributions to understanding the relationship between sound and our environment, and its influence on our perception.

R. Murray Schafer's concept of "soundscape" refers to the total acoustic environment of a particular place, encompassing natural sounds, human activities, and man-made noises. Schafer advocated preservation the soundscape as a crucial cultural and ecological heritage. He believed that the quality of our auditory environment is essential for the well-being of individuals and communities.

In his work *The Tuning of the World*, Schafer emphasized the importance of listening to the sounds around us and how these sounds shape our experience of the world. He encouraged a more mindful approach to sound, akin to the attention we give to visual aesthetics.

Additionally, Schafer was involved in developing the term "schizophonia," which refers to the separation between sound and its source. With the rise of technology and the ability to separate sound from its origin, Schafer explored how this phenomenon changes our relationship with sound.

In summary, R. Murray Schafer made an invaluable contribution to the awareness of sound in our environment and its impact on our well-being. His work led to a better understanding of the role of sound in our lives and influenced various fields, including music, ecology, and sound studies.

Schafer's ideas on the importance of sound in our natural environment have profoundly influenced my own understanding and appreciation of sound. His concept of "soundscape" has opened my ears to the rich and diverse sounds of nature, and the realization that these sounds are not merely random noise but rather advanced communication tools between different elements of the ecosystem.

Sound in nature serves as a powerful means of communication among animals, plants, and even ecosystems. From birdsong indicating territory to marine mammal sounds representing a complex form of interaction, I have come to understand that sound is a deeply rooted language in the natural world.

Observing how animals use sound for warnings, mating rituals, and even finding food has made me realize that sound is more than a pleasant background melody. It is a crucial element of ecological dynamics, allowing different species to survive, collaborate, and thrive.

This new perception of sound has enriched my approach to music and timbre. It has inspired my creative process by incorporating the diversity and complexity of natural sounds into my musical compositions. Nature creates a symphony of sounds, and I too have begun to see sound as a powerful form of expression that extends beyond human communication.

Essentially, Murray Schafer's work has not only refined my hearing but also broadened my awareness of the profound relationship between sound and nature. He has encouraged me to listen to my environment with renewed appreciation and to channel this inspiration into my artistic expressions.

Nature, with its infinite diversity and enchanting beauty, has inspired countless composers throughout the ages. These masters of music have been guided by the sounds, rhythms, and atmospheres of the natural world to create works that establish a deep connection between music and the environment in which we live.

For example, the German composer Ludwig van Beethoven, renowned for his love of nature walks, created his Sixth Symphony, also known as the "Pastoral," as a sublime example of how nature influenced his creative mind. With movements like "Awakening of Cheerful Feelings upon Arrival in the Country" and "Storm," Beethoven transports the listener directly into the heart of the natural world, reflecting both the serene joy and the power of a stormy day.

This illustrates how nature has been a rich source of inspiration for composers, translating the sounds and atmospheres of their environment into timeless musical masterpieces. Nature provides a treasure trove of sounds that invite composers to explore the limits of their creativity and offer listeners a profound experience that resonates with the world around them.

During my studies in composition at the Conservatoire of Amsterdam, Olivier Messiaen's *"Catalogue d'Oiseaux"* profoundly influenced my artistic development. Completed by Messiaen between 1956 and 1958, this composition is a masterpiece that delves into the various sounds and song groups of birds. This musical exploration of the natural world fascinated me and opened new perspectives on how sounds can be integrated into compositions.

Messiaen, known for his use of modes, rhythmic complexity, and synesthetic approach to music, created with *"Catalogue d'Oiseaux"* a sonic journey that takes the listener to the heart of nature. The detailed representation of bird songs, with their rich harmonies and complex rhythms, encouraged me to explore and incorporate natural sounds more deeply into my own compositions.

The aspect of "stream" in Bach's name adds a fascinating layer to the interpretation of Johann Sebastian Bach's music. The German word "Bach" means "stream" or "brook," and whether or not it is a coincidence that the great composer has this surname, it certainly carries a poetic and symbolic element.

Considering the association with a stream, we can view Bach's music as a flow of sounds, moving with clarity, variation, and a constant search for new creative heights. Like a stream winding through landscapes, Bach's music traverses different emotions, structures, and stylistic approaches.

Bach's music is known for its complexity and depth, and the analogy with a stream can help us understand how his compositions develop and connect. A stream might babble gently and then flow and surge. Similarly, the listener experiences diverse emotions and dynamics in Bach's pieces.

Moreover, the stream metaphor can remind us of the timelessness of Bach's work. A stream continues to flow through the seasons, and Bach's music, too, remains relevant and inspiring century after century.

In this interpretation, the name "Bach" not only conveys a surname but also adds a poetic element to how we understand and appreciate his musical legacy. It highlights the ongoing movement, depth, and vitality of his musical creations, inviting us to experience his music as a continuous flow of beauty and meaning.

I have always harbored a deep passion for boats, driven by a profound desire for adventure and freedom on the open sea. My lifelong dream was to sail the vast oceans, feel the wind in my sails, and wander wherever the horizon would lead me. Although I never had the chance to set sail on the ocean, for a time, I cherished a beautiful 38-foot sailboat, which stood by me as a faithful companion in my ardent yearning for the sea.

But before I could chart a course for my oceanic dream, I found myself surrounded by the calm waters of a picturesque canal, where I lived on a majestic houseboat for 25 years. Its gleaming hull reflected the sun's rays, while its sleek, white silhouette carried the promise of adventure and discovery.

Step into the heart of the houseboat and be enchanted by its warm and inviting atmosphere. The loft-style living room is bathed in soft light filtering through the portholes, creating a sense of serenity and tranquility. Comfortable seating invites relaxation, while artistic decorations and colorful accents bring vibrancy and character to the interior.

As you wander through the spacious quarters, you'll be captivated by the stunning views of the tranquil water before you. Behind the windows stretches an infinite horizon, a canvas of timeless beauty that nourishes and inspires the soul. This is not merely a boat; it is a sanctuary, a refuge where the world's worries dissolve into the gentle lapping of the water and the soft, caressing breeze.

But the true highlight of the houseboat is the superb terrace at the front, where you can enjoy breathtaking views of the surrounding nature reserve. As the sun sets on the horizon, the sky is painted in shades of pink and orange, creating an enchanting spectacle that delights the senses each evening.

During the summer months, the crystal-clear canal water offers a refreshing oasis for swimming, while in winter, the surrounding canals transform into a magical ice paradise for my polar bear rituals. The sound of migratory birds flying overhead fills the air with a symphony of sounds, while the peace of nature nourishes and inspires the soul.

And as night falls and the stars twinkle in the sky, the atmosphere on the houseboat is further enriched by the enchanting melodies of the nightingale. The sweetness of its song lulls me to sleep, filling the night with a symphony of soothing sounds. The nightingale, a faithful companion in the silent hours of the night, reminds me of the deep connection between music and natural sounds, a central theme in my exploration of the healing power of sound.

Over the course of these 25 years of my life, I have developed a profound affinity for the power and beauty of water. Through sailing, the sound of the waves, the rhythmic play of the tides, and the serene silence I experienced have created a poetic symphony within me.

As I maneuvered my boat through calm waters, my biodynamic craniosacral rhythm seemed to unite with the natural cadence of the ocean. It felt as though my inner rhythms were merging with those of the sea, and in this unity, a moment of pure serenity emerged.

The salty air of the atmosphere seems imbued with a melody that is inaudible to the human ear but profoundly penetrating to my soul. This experience of connection with the elements weaves a harmonious pattern: it appeals not only to the physical senses but also reveals a deep, spiritual understanding of my relationship with nature.

These personal experiences, imbued with the soothing and inspiring power of water, have led me to reflect on the deeper connection between nature and our own creative expressions. It seems that the elements of the natural world, in all their simplicity and complexity, speak a universal language resonant with the deeper tones of my life's narrative.

The perspectives I have gained from the worlds of advertising, retail environments, restaurants, and nature have profoundly influenced my approach to music as a means of communication. If there is a clear communicative significance attributed to sound in all these contexts, then it is essential that my music also focuses on effective communication.

Instead of directly selling a product, I aim to captivate and motivate people to engage with my story through my music. The intelligibility of my music is therefore vital. It is not only the melody but also the clarity and expressiveness of the sounds I choose that invite the listener to delve deeper into my musical narrative.

Just as a well-designed advertisement or an atmosphere in a restaurant can inspire and engage people, I want my music to have a similar impact. The goal is not merely to please but to create an emotional resonance that lingers in the listener's consciousness. By viewing my compositions as a form of subtle yet powerful communication, I can connect with my audience on a deeper level.

This approach allows me to elevate the listening experience, where each sound, melody, and rhythm is carefully chosen to tell a meaningful story. My music becomes not only an artistic expression but also an invitation to embark together on a journey, with its communicative power serving as a bridge between my creativity and the listener.

CHAPTER 9

HARMONIES OF THE WORLD

$\mathcal{M}$usic, it seems, is much more than an arrangement of sounds that reach our ears. It is an art form deeply rooted in the energy around us, guiding and nourishing us in ways that transcend our everyday understanding. Can we surpass the limitations of our senses and open ourselves to the subtle forces surrounding music? Is there a free, invisible but always present energy that cannot be created by human hands but exists eternally, sometimes obscured by a layer of ignorance, waiting to be discovered?

Ask these questions to someone facing famine or war, and you will likely receive a dismissive look. In the harsh reality of physical hardships, such abstract contemplations may seem like a luxury. But isn't it precisely in the most difficult circumstances that the power of music manifests most clearly? It may be the memories of melodies that bring comfort in times of sorrow or the rhythms that create a sense of community amid chaos.

My travels serve as an inexhaustible source of inspiration in my ongoing quest to understand the essence of music and its healing power. Each destination has brought me not only new melodies and rhythms but also opened doors to diverse cultures, traditions, and spiritual beliefs. This rich diversity of experiences has broadened my musical horizons and deepened my understanding of the profound meaning of music.

Over the years, these journeys have exposed me to various cultures that, despite their rich history and deep spiritual traditions, face difficult circumstances. From expansive reserves to remote villages around the world, I have encountered communities that preserve their unique cultural identity despite poverty, marginalization, and migration.

It is striking to see how music proves to be a powerful and universal support for these communities in their quest for survival and preservation of their heritage. In the warm sounds of traditional songs and the rhythms of ritual dances, they find not only a form of artistic expression but also a source of comfort, resilience, and community bonds.

Whether it is the thunderous drum circles of indigenous tribes in North America, the captivating songs in remote African villages, or the harmonious convergence of instruments in Asia, again and again, I have observed the essential role of music in weaving a network of community support and spiritual connection.

These experiences have deepened my perspective on music, and I have come to understand that the power of sounds and melodies goes beyond mere aesthetic pleasure. In the most pressing circumstances, music acts as a balm for the soul, a force that alleviates the burdens of daily life and also bridges the gap between generations and cultures.

My goal has become to share and explore this interconnectedness of music with daily life and its spiritual dimension. In every chord, every drumbeat, every melody, lies a story of resilience, perseverance, and hope. These travels have not only enriched me musically but have also led me to a deeper understanding of the healing power of music in the most diverse corners of the world.

In a modest neighborhood in Lima, Peru, where daily life was marked by simplicity and poverty, I witnessed a remarkable event that revealed the healing power of music. Far from any war devastation, it was an ordinary and impoverished neighborhood that nevertheless had a story of connection and hope to tell.

After enjoying a delicious meal with friends at a typical Peruvian restaurant, adorned with plastic tablecloths and simple decorations, we basked in the sun on the terrace. The ceviche fish soup was delightful, and we were charmed by the local atmosphere of the restaurant. Amidst our lively conversation and laughter, my attention was suddenly drawn to a distant sound. I apologized to my friends and descended from the terrace, curious about the source of this sound.

In the narrow alleys of this modest neighborhood, I discovered a local musician playing a simple melody on his worn guitar. Residents of all ages were enchanted by the melody and began to sing and move spontaneously. This powerful music of hope briefly revived the neighborhood. Children momentarily forgot their worries, adults found comfort, and the elderly shared moments of joy.

This musical intervention, far from the ravages of war, reminded us that music has the ability to connect communities and offer comfort in the simplest forms of daily life.

In our search for meaning and connection, we cannot overlook the role of music as a gateway to a deeper reality. It is not just about listening with our ears but also about feeling with our beings, opening ourselves to the invisible forces around us. Perhaps it is in those moments of silence, between the notes, that we can discover the true essence of life and the elusive forces of music.

During my travels across Africa, I was told an enchanting

story that not only stimulated my senses but also inspired my creative spirit to compose an original piece. It possessed a depth of wisdom that our modern civilization might envy. This story opened my eyes to the realization that true knowledge is often hidden behind doors we have yet to unlock. I came to understand that acquiring genuine knowledge urges us to expand our minds and look beyond the confines of our familiar ways of thinking. "Seeing is believing," but in this particular story, I discovered the power of believing before seeing.

In the heart of the Dogon Valley, where the sun beat mercilessly on the parched earth and the thirsty crops yearned desperately for rain, lay a small village named Tamani. Tamani meant "hope" in the Dogon language, and it was precisely what the inhabitants needed in these times of unprecedented drought.

The harvests had been poor, and the village was suffering under the weight of an impending famine. The elders remembered tales of times when rains were plentiful, but now it seemed as if the heavens had withdrawn their grace. Water sources were drying up, and fields were turning into barren expanses.

However, in these desperate times, a new sound emerged in Tamani. A young woman named Amina discovered an ancient tradition from the time of her grandparents: songs to appease the rain gods. These songs had long been forgotten, buried under layers of modernity and despair.

Determined to learn more, Amina began to study the songs with the village elders. She gathered the children, the elderly, and everyone in between to participate in these ancestral rituals. The sounds of the songs filled the dry air, resonated through the valley, and rose to the sky as pleas for redemption.

Amazingly, in the days that followed, changes began to occur. The dry wind suddenly brought clouds, and the unimaginable happened: rain appeared. Astonished, the village watched as the earth opened up and the parched soil absorbed the water like a gift from the gods.

The songs became a daily practice in Tamani. It seemed that the melodies had a direct connection to the clouds above them. Crops began to grow, flowers appeared, and the once-dry riverbed started to flow again. The songs had awakened the power of the natural world.

The story of Tamani spread like a breeze across the Dogon Valley. Other villages began to adopt their own songs and rituals, and soon the arid regions became green oases of abundance. People realized that there was more between heaven and earth than they could see and that harmony between humans and nature could be restored through the ancient wisdom of songs.

Tamani, once a symbol of despair, had become a symbol of hope and resilience. The village had demonstrated that in times of adversity, the power of songs and traditions could be the key to restoring balance between humans and nature. And so, under the blessing of rain, the people of Tamani sang their songs of gratitude and renewed hope.

My spiritual journey has always been driven by a profound intention to unravel the mysterious forces present in my music. I believed that by understanding these forces, I would be able to harness them more effectively, with the ultimate goal of resonating deeply with my audience and creating meaningful moments. One of the captivating paths I pursued in this quest for musical magic was rooted in the ancient culture of the Sioux Native American medicine circle.

This ancient culture provided me with profound insights that I wanted to integrate into the music I created. These discoveries were not for me a mere addition to the esoteric sounds of New Age music, but rather an authentic quest for the deeper meaning of music and its capacity to forge spiritual connections.

In my search for a deeper connection between music and

spirituality, I sought to weave the valuable lessons of the medicine circle into my compositions and performances. It was an unconventional approach, as I aimed to step away from traditional paths of esoteric music. My goal was to blend the ancient wisdom of the Sioux tribe with contemporary musical expression, believing that the universal language of sound and melody could unlock deeper layers of spiritual experience.

This integration of spiritual discoveries into my musical creations was a personal journey that went beyond mere artistic experimentation. It was a quest for authenticity and an exploration of the limits of what music can mean for the spiritual well-being of the listener. In my musical explorations, I remained true to my own spiritual discoveries, realizing that the true magic of music often lies in its ability to embrace the invisible and uplift the soul, regardless of artistic genres or conventions.

My introduction to this spiritual tradition began with in-depth readings about their rituals, customs, and the deeper significance of the medicine circle. My exploration of the Sioux culture was not only influenced by my own curiosity but also stemmed from the experiences of my violin teacher. She encouraged me to read books about the Sioux, as she had done in her youth. Her passion for the rich and profound traditions of this indigenous community sparked my interest and led me to delve deeply into their culture. What began as a shared interest quickly became a personal journey of understanding and spiritual discovery.

As a child, I had already had a connection with this culture that went beyond the pages of books. My parents lived and worked in the United States for a time, where I, as a child, had been exposed to the rich indigenous traditions. As I write these words, my gaze rests on the beautiful Kachina doll proudly displayed on my studio shelf. A precious memento from my childhood in the United States, where the seed was planted for my subsequent exploration of the deeper layers of spiritual and musical connection. The Kachina doll, with its colorful and symbolic expression, serves as a tangible reminder of the cultural richness I had the privilege to experience, shaping and inspiring my journey.

Later in my young adult life, driven by a deep desire to deepen my knowledge and immerse myself in the ancient culture of the medicine circle, I met a woman who had been married to a member of the Sioux tribe. She took me under her wing and introduced me to their rituals and wisdom. This experience was crucial to my understanding of the spiritual dimensions of music.

In the heart of North America, amid the vast plains and rich history of the Sioux tribe, I found my way to the Hunkpati tribe. My quest for answers within this ancient culture brought me closer to the soul of this community over the years, and eventually, I had the privilege of being their guest.

Throughout history, the Hunkpati, a branch of the Sioux tribe, have cultivated a rich and deeply rooted culture. As indigenous people of North America, they have a unique connection with the land and have preserved their traditional way of life and spiritual beliefs for centuries. The name "Hunkpati" itself carries meaning, translating as "those who live on a great foot." This title reflects their historical relationship with the vast land and their skills as nomadic hunters and gatherers.

The Hunkpati have a profound spiritual connection with nature, considering elements such as earth, air, fire, and water as sacred. Their beliefs are intertwined with the cycles of nature, and many of their rituals and ceremonies focus on honoring these spiritual elements.

A remarkable aspect of Hunkpati culture is their use of the

medicine circle, a sacred symbol often used for spiritual and ceremonial purposes. The medicine circle represents the cycles of life, seasons, and the connection between all living beings. It is a powerful tool for reflection and guidance, frequently involved in rituals focused on healing and balance.

The experiences during my visits to the Hunkpati tribe constitute a vibrant chapter of my personal journey. During one particular ritual, where the air was filled with the scent of burning sage and the moving sounds of drums and chants touched the soul, I witnessed the deeply rooted spiritual practices of this tribe.

In the circular arena, a sanctuary where the community gathered to dance and sing under the blazing sun, an enchanting dance ceremony unfolded, infused with vibrant colors, impressive costumes, and the moving sounds of musicians.

The musicians, arranged in small groups under the shelter, created a lively spectacle. Armed with large drums, each group played a single drum, surrounded by percussionists enriching the sounds with ritual chants. Amidst the musical activity, tribe members danced in their beautiful costumes adorned with feathers and shimmering colors, indifferent to the heat. The dancers moved in a circle at the center of the arena, guided by the pulsating rhythm of the drums and chants. I was mesmerized by this total, colorful spectacle.

Later, I learned that these colors were not only aesthetic but also carried a deeper spiritual meaning. They represented frequencies, much like music, vibrations resonating with the essence of the universe. Thus, the dance became not only a physical expression but also a harmonic resonance with the cosmos, where dancers and musicians came together to create this spiritual symbiosis. This experience enriched my understanding of music, spirituality, and community, and remains a powerful memory of the intertwining of music and culture within the Sioux tribe.

The ritual, steeped in symbolism and rich traditions, culminated in these colorful dances where the participants' feet seemed to offer a gentle massage to Mother Earth. The dancers, clad in their beautiful traditional costumes, executed each movement with grace and intention, and I felt the power of their connection with the earth and the spirits.

One of the most striking moments came when, unexpectedly, an eagle feather fell from a costume to the ground, causing a wave of panic among the participants. Quickly, some senior members of the tribe formed a circle around the feather. With chants, dances, and ritual gestures, they sought to counter any desecration.

I later learned the deeper significance of this unexpected incident. That very night, a grandmother from the village had passed away. The intensity of the ritual, with its music, chants, and drums, proved to be a powerful support for the tribe in their mourning process and in guiding the soul of the deceased grandmother to the other world.

These experiences illuminated the profound role of music, chants, and rituals not only as artistic expressions but also as deeply rooted pillars of spiritual power and community cohesion. In the most challenging moments, these elements offer comfort and guidance, and I keenly felt the invaluable importance of music woven into the very fabric of daily life for the Sioux tribe.

The ritual we observed took place under the guise of a competition, a stratagem necessitated by government restrictions on traditional practices. This supposed competition judged elements such as costumes, musical performance, and dance movements as if it were merely an artistic showcase. I was deeply troubled that the essence of the ceremony—

honoring Mother Earth and expressing gratitude to the ancestors—had to be a pretext to meet legal constraints.

The tragedy became even more poignant when I realized that this community, despite having the right to reside on their own land—the reservation—after a painful history of displacement and return, still struggled with the challenges stemming from the presence of casinos and low taxes on alcohol and tobacco. The reservation, once lost and then reclaimed, was now riddled with temptations that made the local population vulnerable to addiction to alcohol and cigarettes. It was a bitter irony that their spiritual rituals, intended to foster harmony and support in the face of life's trials, had to hide behind an artistic facade to survive in a world that eroded their self-esteem and undermined their traditions.

In the streets of Alexandria, Egypt, I embarked on a quest to find a darbouka, a traditional percussion instrument deeply rooted in the local musical heritage. The streets buzzed with a cacophony of sounds, from the roar of engines to the chatter of people conversing in narrow alleyways. The sun beat down mercilessly on my skin as I navigated the labyrinthine streets, its warm rays palpable on my face and arms. The heat seemed to amplify the scent of spices, saturating the air with the intoxicating aromas of cinnamon, cumin, and fresh herbs.

Soon after, I encountered a local resident who directed me to a secluded alleyway, away from the hustle and bustle of tourist spots. In this dimly lit alley, I discovered a treasure trove of darboukas of various sizes, all waiting patiently to be played. The walls were adorned with vibrant graffiti, and the floor was dotted with colorful rugs and souvenir stalls. The sounds of the city faded here, replaced by the soft tinkling of darboukas hanging from hooks on the walls.

Despite the language barrier, I communicated through gestures and smiles as I tried out the different darboukas. My fingers quickly found a rhythm that resonated with my soul, and I began to play with a gentle, hypnotic cadence. Before I knew it, my music attracted the attention of locals sipping tea nearby. They joined in, clapping and singing in unison, transforming our little alleyway into a joyous session of musical improvisation filled with music and laughter.

The smiling faces of the local residents welcomed me as I mingled with them, my fingers dancing on the drumheads of the darboukas. Their eyes sparkled with joy as they clapped and sang in harmony, their beaming faces illuminated by the soft afternoon sunlight. In this moment of connection and joy, surrounded by the warmth and scents of Alexandria, I felt more alive than ever. I had truly found the soul of the city, hidden in the melodies of its music and the warmth of its people.

At the heart of my artistic journey lie these stories that have ignited my thirst to understand the deeper origins and purposes of music. These narratives have had a transformative effect on my perception of music, shifting my quest for personal recognition and ego gratification towards a nobler purpose: to make a humanitarian contribution to the community with the talent bestowed upon me at birth.

This shift in my approach has led me to reflect on the impact of my compositions and performances. No longer solely focused on personal success, I aspire to keep in mind a deeper goal: how can my music serve as a powerful instrument for positive change? How can I, beyond entertaining my listeners, provide them with an energetic charge that enables them to face the world with renewed courage, after my concerts?

These reflections have given rise to particular questions that permeate my thoughts and keep me awake during the quiet hours of the night. Questions about the limits of music's influence on the human mind and soul. Can music even have therapeutic effects? In my quest for answers, one certainty remains with me: the recognition that we do not know everything. The mysteries of music's power might well be within reach, ready to be discovered and unveiled.

As an artist, I feel compelled to dig deeper, to elevate my creative expression to a level where it not only pleases the senses but also carries a deeper meaning and impact. The stories that have shaped me serve as a compass on this journey of discovery, and I hope that my musical path not only reflects my personal growth but also contributes to the well-being of the listener.

CHAPTER 10

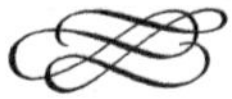

THE SILENCE OF RELIGION

The evening descended like a soft blanket over the city. The streets were filled with the whispers of the wind and the muted sound of footsteps on the pavement. In the intimate silence of my study, surrounded by books and the soft glow of a single lamp, I began to reflect on the meaning of religion in my life. My journey had started with firm beliefs and traditional paths. Religion, as I had known it before, was made up of principles.

But the silence in music slowly began to capture my attention, like a resting point between notes as powerful as the tones themselves. The symphony of faith took a turn when I discovered the beauty of the space between the notes, the moments of silence at the heart of the music. I recognized the voice of silence, a deep and mysterious resonance that spoke more than words ever could.

I found my way to silence by listening to different types of music: from subdued classical compositions to the meditative sounds of distant lands. In these moments of contemplation, I discovered a new dimension of spirituality, a transcendent experience beyond dogmas and rituals.

Religion, I realized, was more than just rules and prescriptions. It was a living, breathing entity, resonating in the silence, in the space between the notes of life. Silence opened the door to an intimate dialogue with the divine, a dialogue not dictated by words but by the subtle depths of the soul. Instead of clinging to a specific doctrine, I began to shape my spirituality around the silence in music, a personal journey, an exploration that led me to a deeper understanding of myself and my relationship with the divine.

I let silence guide me, like a companion on an inner journey. Churches, mosques, and temples were no longer just seen as sacred places bound by dogmas but as spaces where silence can resonate, where the spiritual symphony of life can manifest.

Deeply immersed in the silence of my study, the ancient wisdom of the Old Testament reached me: "Be still, and know that I am God." These words, first heard during my catechism lessons, took on a new meaning through my musical experiences. As I surrounded myself with the tones of my favorite musical pieces, I understood that divine silence was not simply a command to speak or meditate quietly but an invitation to consider silence as a sanctuary. God speaks through music, through the moments when notes disappear, and only silence remains.

In music, I discovered that the same divine silence manifests between crescendos and decrescendos, between harmonies and dissonances. It is a silence not confined to one faith or interpretation. It extends to all sounds that can touch the soul. Divine silence has become a universal language, understood by those who listen with the heart.

My catechism lessons had spoken of a God who spoke with a thunderous voice and powerful works, but now I understand that God also speaks through the whispers of silence. It is an invitation to remain still, to listen, and to experience that the divine is not confined to dogmas and doctrines but to a transcendent presence found everywhere and nowhere.

In my musical journey, I discovered that "Be still, and know that I am God" did not mean that God was distant but rather that God revealed Himself in the deepest silence of the heart. It is an invitation to go beyond words and concepts, to feel the essence of the divine in the rest between the notes of existence.

My quest to explore the meaning of silence led me to India, where ancient wisdom speaks of true religion found in the depth of silence. In the shadow of majestic temples, beneath the branches of ancient trees, I realized that there was a universal truth hidden in the silence deeply rooted in Indian spiritual traditions.

"Within silence, you find true religion," wise men and women told me. It was more than a teaching; it was an invitation to embark on an inner journey, to go beyond the external façade of rituals and temples, and to discover the true essence revealed in silence.

This belief was reflected in the meditative practices deeply ingrained in Indian culture. Through yoga, contemplation, and deep silence, one seeks a direct connection with the divine.

The Ganges, the sacred river flowing like vital blood through the country, whispers tales of ancient wisdom. Ashrams, secluded retreats amid lush nature, serve as sanctuaries for those wishing to explore the depth of divine silence.

I found myself on the banks of sacred rivers, surrounded by the sounds of mantras and the fragrance of incense. Here, I understood that true religion is not confined to religious rituals but rather represents an inner state of consciousness. It is the silence that resonates in the human heart, a silence that speaks of a deeper unity beyond external differences.

In India, I discovered that true religion in silence was not exclusive to a single faith or culture. It was a universal truth understood and honored by various spiritual traditions. The

Hindu sage, the Buddhist monk, The Islamic poet —all speak the language of silence, the language of universal divinity. Reflecting on my journey, I realized that silence was not only a personal discovery but also a bridge between cultures and beliefs.

For several days, I sailed on a boat gliding through the picturesque backwaters of Kerala, in southern India, a masterpiece of wood and reeds. The silence on board was only interrupted by the soothing splash of water against the boat and the gentle murmur of the wind through the lush reed beds. Amid this serene backdrop of abundant nature, I began to grasp the deeper meaning behind the Zen expression: "Only in calm water can you see your face."

In the contemplative stillness of the calm water around me, I saw not only my own reflection but also the reflection of the natural beauty surrounding me. The trees along the banks mirrored like living paintings on the smooth water's surface, while the sky seemed to form an infinite dome in the sparkling waters. But it was not just the visual spectacle that enchanted me. As I stood on the deck, I could hear the melodies of numerous singing birds in the trees, a symphony of natural beauty enveloping my soul. There were also the rice fields with workers in traditional attire. The sound of their voices blended with the rustling of the reeds and the gentle splash of water. The smell of freshly cooked fish from nearby villages filled my nostrils, mingled with the sweet fragrance of lotus flowers.

The days on the boat became a time of total immersion in the lush natural landscapes. I was in harmony with the environment, surrounded by the abundant beauty of Mother Nature. Each moment was a celebration of life, a reminder of the boundless splendor of the world around us.

As the days passed, I gained a deeper understanding of the meaning of Zen. It was only in the gentle stillness, in the inner silence, that I could clearly perceive my own essence, free from the ripples of worries and distractions that cloud the mirror—a reminder of the importance of serenity in daily life, an invitation to calm the waves of the mind and uncover the deeper truths of the self.

In the evening, when we docked at the edge of the rice fields, we were invited to a delightful meal, prepared with the simple yet exquisite culinary skills of our cook. As I stood on the deck just before sunset, I witnessed a remarkable event that deeply moved me.

From afar, an old man approached us slowly in his wooden canoe, alone on the calm waters. It seemed like a dream as he glided past our boat and stopped at the edge of a group of banana trees. There, he took a few bunches, placed them in his boat, and continued his tranquil journey.

The rice fields extended beyond the shore, a sea of green shimmering under the warm orange glow of the setting sun. The banana trees swayed gently in the evening breeze, their dark green leaves a vibrant contrast to the otherwise peaceful surroundings.

The old man's canoe was almost black, polished by years of use on the calm waters of the backwaters. Its smooth wooden surface reflected the colors of the surroundings like a mirror, blending into the serene beauty of the nature that surrounded it.

The waters were perfectly smooth, barely disturbed by the gentle splash of the boat and the slight rustling of the wind through the reed beds. The reflection of the setting sun on the calm water created an enchanting display of colors, the sky seeming to merge with the surface of the lake.

I was completely overwhelmed by the serenity of the old man and felt in perfect harmony with the silence of the night. Catching a fleeting glimpse of his face, I experienced a deep sense of peace and inspiration. His gaze seemed to capture mine, and I was enchanted by the silence he brought with him.

I will forever carry the image of the old man with me, especially during moments of agitation. It reminds me that amidst the chaos of life, there is always a possible oasis of calm within oneself.

During those days on the waters of southern India, I found peace in the silence and came to understand the essence of our spiritual quest from the religious teachings we have been given.

It was in Tiruvannamalai, a town in the state of Tamil Nadu in southeastern India, that I had an extraordinary experience of silence. The morning sun cast a gentle glow on the landscape as I set out on the long hike to the summit of the hill, heading towards the cave of Sri Ramana Maharshi. The narrow, winding path led me through an enchanting landscape, surrounded by dry trees, tall grasses, and the promise of silence, high above the city.

Each step felt like a journey through time, following in the footsteps of this sage, carving my own path amidst the beautiful nature that accompanied his daily contemplation journey. The narrow, winding path led me to the heart of my own inner quest. As time went on, moving away from the city, a distance grew between me and the noise of daily life, the songs of birds and the rustling of leaves slowly replacing the city's background noise.

The purity of the air allowed me to breathe in the refreshing scent of nature. The cave of Sri Ramana Maharshi gradually appeared, a modest opening in the rocks that served as a refuge for inner reflection. A sacred place, imbued with the energy of many seekers who had come before me in search of silence. This physical distance from the city also gradually took me further from the prosaic mental gap obscuring the search for the transcendent.

Entering the cave, I felt the serenity of the place, a dimension deeply cherished by those who had sought and found it. I deserved this feeling of happiness as a result of the physical effort of the ascent and the inner journey. Sitting in the cave, overlooking the valley and the distant city, I gently slipped into a state of meditation.

In the cave of Sri Ramana Maharshi, high above the world, I was finally rewarded for my search effort, no longer an abstraction of beautiful literary words but a tangible sensation of happiness.

Sri Ramana Maharshi had lived there in contemplation, away from the trivial distractions of daily life. The cave offered little comfort: no bed, no table, no chairs. It was a simple space that spoke of renunciation of material possessions, a conscious choice to undertake the inner journey without the distractions of material abundance. The message of the great master was a spiritual legacy of reflection, personal stripping away, and simplicity.

I felt a connection with the sage who had once sat there, his gaze delving into the depths of his own consciousness. In the silence of the cave, I understood that his journey was a quest for the essential, the inner essence that forms the heart of all experiences. Sri Ramana Maharshi's lifestyle, his fasting, and his limited possessions testified to a deep understanding that true essence is not dependent on material abundance.

I found no answers to the questions but rather a silent guidance to where the true treasure lay. It became clear to me that believing in a specific doctrine was not necessary to understand the universal essence. Here, far from dogmas and rituals, I discovered the common ground on which all religions lay their foundation.

I understand that well-being evolves from a simple appreciation of tones to a holistic awareness of the healing power of silence. Just as the silence in Sri Ramana Maharshi's cave could calm and uplift the spirit, so too can the silence between the notes of my music create a space for inner peace and contemplation.

The appeal of ancient musical styles transcends the boundaries of time, culture, and religion, and their goal of drawing closer to the divine is often imbued with a universal desire for spiritual connection. These musical forms serve as timeless channels that enable humanity to transcend earthly limits and experience a deeper understanding of the divine.

In the fluid melodies of these traditions, many of which have been passed down through generations, the call to the divine seems to resonate without being confined to specific doctrines or dogmas. Music acts as a universal language that unites people in their common quest for transcendence.

Thus, when we listen to the ancestral melodies passed down to us, we are not only experiencing the music itself but also the timeless quest for the divine that resonates through the notes and silence. It is an endless journey, one that propels the soul and reminds us of the possibility of drawing closer to the unknown, the divine, through the sounds and silence of music.

In my exploration of Flemish polyphony, the subtly measured silences between the notes form an essential dimension for unraveling the deeper layers of this musical tradition. The lush harmonies and complex structures of Flemish polyphony are imbued with a serene atmosphere, a common unspoken invitation to composers and performers alike to understand the meaning of this space.

The Franco-Flemish tradition, renowned for the works of composers such as Josquin des Prez, Guillaume Dufay, and Ockeghem, invites deep contemplation of the space between the notes. As I immerse myself in this music, I realize that it is not merely about reproducing the notes on paper but also about grasping the intention behind each tone, the composer's breath resonating within the contained void.

In the muted moments between contrapuntal voices, I sense the composer's creative breath. Silence forms a backdrop against which the tones are sketched, and the art lies in understanding the nuances of this space. Flemish polyphony composers use silence as an artistic tool, allowing the listener not only to hear the tones but also to feel the space between them.

For me, interpreting this is a liturgical quest to capture and understand the subtleties of timing and expression that give music its unique character. It's a process of listening to the composer's breath, feeling the space in which each note comes to life, and connecting with the deeper intention of the religious message.

In the quest for the divine in music, a beautiful conversation unfolds between the past and the present. The tender strings of the viola da gamba, the lute, and the viola d'amore a chiavi (nyckelharpa) converse with the contemporary sounds of the modern piano, double bass, and drums. A symbiosis emerges where ancient music and jazz intersect, an eternal play that transcends the boundaries of time and tradition.

The melancholic tones of the viola da gamba resonate with the contemporary sounds of the piano, while the lute and double bass create a rhythmic interplay that infuses ancient melodies with new dynamics. the viola d'amore a chiavi , with its unique resonance, adds an enchanting nuance to the ensemble, serving as a bridge between the ancient and modern sound worlds.

The rhythmic drive of the drums introduces a contemporary cadence to the harmonic complexity of ancient compositions. It's a meeting of two worlds, where the depth of ancient music intertwines with the improvisation and freedom of jazz. The double bass, as a unifying force, weaves a sonic tapestry with modern instruments, where past and present harmoniously merge.

This fusion of sounds is not merely a combination of instruments but also a reflection of the ongoing quest for the divine through the ages. Musicians, with their diverse instruments and backgrounds, participate in a cosmic conversation where time and space blur.

This musical journey is a celebration of diversity, an ode to the timeless power of music that builds bridges between different eras and cultures. It's a reminder that the quest for the divine in music is not tied to a specific moment or place but rather to a continuous flow of creative expression.

Thus, the musical space is filled with the sound of the old and the new dancing together, an enchanting symphony of sounds that speaks to the soul. In the fusion of ancient music and jazz, an eternal conversation unfolds—a dialogue where the sensitive strings of the past and the modern rhythms of the present come together, complementing each other, and continuing the endless journey towards the divine in music.

Through my collaboration with ancient Sufi music and the lofty verses of Rumi, a new dimension of understanding emerges regarding the silence between the words. The instrumentation, composed of the oud, ney, and yaylı tambur, offers a refined complement to this spiritual dialogue, where timeless sounds harmonize with the modern tones of the piano and the the viola d'amore a chiavi.

The light tones of the oud transport me to a timeless atmosphere where the soul of the music merges with Rumi's mystical teachings. The strings of the oud build a bridge between centuries: today's music and the profound wisdom of the past. In this fusion of sounds, a spiritual conversation rises, transcending the limits of time and culture.

The whispering melodies of the ney add an ethereal dimension to the mystical dialogue. The rich sounds of this ancient flute evoke a sense of contemplation and inner silence, allowing the music to be not only heard but also felt at a deeper level: a meeting of the old and the new.

The resonances of the yaylı tambur add a terrestrial depth to the ensemble, and the sound of this bowed instrument weaves a refined tapestry of harmony and emotion. The yaylı tambur, with its rich tonal colors, enhances the subtleties of silence between the tones, thus adding a deeper meaning to the musical conversation.

In this mystical interaction, a dialogue emerges with modern instruments such as the piano, percussion, the viola d'amore a chiavi . The versatility of the piano introduces a contemporary harmonic structure to antiquity.

Together, these instruments create a fascinating blend of sounds: the silence between words and notes speaks an unspoken language. It is a journey where the mystical past intertwines with the modern present, and where silence serves as a sacred space in which the essence of the music unfolds.

The discovery of shared inspiration in Indian ragas opens a new chapter in my musical exploration. The rich melodies and reflective silences of the ragas offer a different perspective on the meaning of musical silence. This ancient tradition speaks a universal language.

My continued pursuit of playing Indian ragas leads me on a deep spiritual journey: each of these pieces serves as a gateway to different emotional and spiritual dimensions. The morning ragas, with their soft sounds and melodic patterns, resonate with the freshness of a new day. The music reflects the awakening of nature, and I feel a connection with the essence of life.

As the hours progress, the atmosphere shifts to the afternoon ragas, where the music takes on an energetic and vibrant tone. I sense the flow of creative energy manifesting in the complex structures of the ragas. The melodic ornaments and rhythmic patterns challenge my skills as a musician, inviting me to dive deeply into the realm of musical expression.

At sunset, with the evening ragas, deeper emotions and contemplation come to the forefront. The music becomes more intense, with slow and captivating movements that induce a meditative state in both the listener and the musician. The raga serves as a bridge between the human and the divine, guiding the tones on a journey through the soul.

The night ragas represent the pinnacle of this spiritual journey. In the deep silence of the night, the music comes to life with a mystical force. The complexity of the structures reaches its zenith, and the melodies seem to transcend the limits of the tangible. It is an experience that makes the connection with the divine palpable, with the music acting as a channel to transcendental energy.

The structure of Indian ragas is remarkably complex. Each raga has its specific scale, melodic contours, and performance time. The improvisational nature of the genre adds an additional dimension to musical expression, making each performance unique. It requires not only technical skill but also a profound emotional and spiritual commitment to convey the true essence of the raga.

The connection between Indian ragas and the divine is deeply rooted in India's spiritual traditions. Ragas are considered a means to achieve spiritual unity and create harmony between the individual self and universal consciousness. Performing this music leads me to a higher presence, a creative energy transmitted through the ages.

In each note, each melodic twist, and each silence between tones, a sacred space emerges where divine creative energy resonates. I participate in an ancient tradition of spiritual exploration and expression, where music serves as a bridge between the human soul and the divine. The complexity of ragas becomes an invitation to delve deeply, and in this exploration, I discover an infinite source of inspiration and meaning.

In my interactions with the kalimba, balafon, or kora in African music, a similar universal resonance is revealed. The subtle sounds of these traditional instruments transport me to distant lands, where music is not merely an artistic expression but also a spiritual journey. It is a meeting with cultures that, despite geographical distances, share the same language of emotion and connection.

In the global harmonies of musical traditions, a dialogue emerges in which the essence of silence is understood and shared. It is a celebration of the diversity of human expression, where music serves as a universal medium to communicate emotions, thoughts, and spirituality. In these intercultural conversations, a rich pallet of sounds emerges, where silence is not only heard but also felt as a binding force among all the musical voices of the world.

My journey through world music has also led me to a unique experience with the didgeridoo, an ancient instrument deeply rooted in Aboriginal Australian culture. The unique sounds of this instrument evoke not only a spiritual connection to the land but also open doors to profound and mystical experiences.

Upon my first listening to the deep resonances of the didgeridoo, I understood that this instrument transcends the limits of sound: it is a journey that transports me to the very heart of the Aboriginal cosmos, a place where sound and spiritual experience merge.

Aborigines do not view the didgeridoo merely as a musical instrument; it is a sacred artifact symbolizing a direct connection with the land and ancestors. Playing the didgeridoo is not just a musical expression for them but a ritual of deep spiritual experience.

The circular breathing technique required to play the didgeridoo creates a constant, hypnotic hum. These repetitive sounds serve as a spiritual mantra, an auditory carpet that transports both the player and the listener into a state of trance and contemplation.

Aborigines know that the didgeridoo captures the sounds of the landscape itself, making the instrument a living memory of the connection between humans and nature. Playing the didgeridoo is their way of harmonizing with the surrounding world and connecting with the spiritual dimensions of life.

During their gatherings where the didgeridoo resonates, a collective experience of profound connection unfolds. The sounds travel through the air and penetrate the heart of the community, creating a collective shift in consciousness. It is a celebration of life, nature, and the ancient wisdom of ancestors.

The didgeridoo has taught me that music can be more than just entertainment; it can be a gateway to a transcendental experience. In the echoes of this termite-eaten acacia tube, I sense the spiritual resonance of a culture living in harmony with the land and its history.

At each concert—whether it's Flemish polyphony, jazzy interpretations of baroque melodies, African music, Australian sounds, Indian ragas, or any other musical journey—extraordinary experiences are regularly etched into my DNA. Each genre, each tonal color, and each melody adds a new chapter to the story of my musical exploration.

In the harmony of Flemish polyphony, I discover the timeless beauty of layered voices reaching like an echo penetrating through the ages. Jazzy interpretations of baroque melodies bring playful freedom and improvisation that stretch my musical boundaries, while African rhythms infuse a pulsating life force into my veins.

Thus, I become a global citizen of sound, a traveler through the musical landscapes of different continents. Australian tones transport me to vast deserts and indigenous stories, while Indian ragas caress my soul with the depth of ancient spiritual traditions. I am able to open doors to empathy and understanding.

Notes transcend the boundaries of geography and culture, speaking a universal language. In the magical moments of fusion with diverse sounds, I feel the essence of humanity illuminate— a reminder that we are all part of the same cosmic song.

Each concert is a pilgrimage, a ritual journey during which my musical self evolves and enriches itself with the treasures of each tradition. Thus, extraordinary experiences are not only written in my DNA but also in the fabric of my musical soul, reshaping and transforming in the light of the various sonic worlds I have the privilege to embrace.

EPILOGUE

The theater curtain is still closed. The audience fills the room with palpable excitement. Just before the concert, the space is enveloped in a serene silence. This silence, spreading like an invisible wave through the space, wraps around us and opens the door to another form of listening. It is a force that transports us to a deeper dimension of concentration. The silence gently lays a veil over us, allowing us to gather our attention and sharpen our senses for the forthcoming musical adventure.

May the silence before the performance remain a sacred space, where we can discover the divine melodies resonating at the heart of our existence.

> "When I am silent,
> I fall into a place where everything is music.
> Everything is made of Love."
> (Rumi)

BIBLIOGRAPHY

OF REFERENCED AND CITED SOURCES

Armour J. Andrew, *Neurocardiology: Anatomical and Functional Principles.*

Byrne Rhonda, *The Secret.*

Cheney Margaret, *Tesla: Man Out of Time.*

Doidge Norman, *The Brain's Way of Healing: Remarkable Discoveries and Recoveries from the Frontiers of Neuroplasticity.*

Dyer Wayne, *Change your Thoughts, change your life: Living the wisdom of the Tao.*

Emoto Masaru, *The Hidden Messages in Water.*

Gibran Khalil, *The Prophet.*

Godwin Joscelyn, *Tradition in Music.*

Griffiths David J., *Introduction to Quantum Mechanics.*

Guthrie Kenneth Sylvan (ed.), *The Pythagorean Sourcebook and Library: An Anthology of Ancient Writings Which Relate to Pythagoras and Pythagorean Philosophy.*

Hallam Susan, Cross Ian, & Thaut Michael (ed.), *The Oxford Handbook of Music Psychology.*

Harford Tim, *Fifty Inventions That Shaped the Modern Economy.*

Herzing Denise, *Profiling nonhuman intelligence: An exercise in developing unbiased tools for describing other "types" of intelligence on earth,* in "Acta Astronautica", vol. 94 Issue 2.

Jung Carl Gustav, *The Archetypes and the Collective Unconscious.*

Krishnamurti Jiddu, *Freedom From the Known.*

LeDoux Joseph, *The Emotional Brain: The Mysterious Underpinnings of Emotional Life.*

Levitin Daniel, *This Is Your Brain on Music: The Science of a Human Obsession.*

Lovelock James, *Gaia Hypothesis.*

Maharshi Ramana, *L'Enseignement de Ramana Maharshi,* vertaling: Eleonore Braitenberg.

Mannes Elena, *The Power of Music: Pioneering Discoveries in the New Science of Song.*

Oliver Sacks, *Musicophilia: Tales of Music and the Brain.*

Rossing Thomas D., *Chladni's Law for Vibrating Plates,* in "American Journal of Physics", Vol. 50 Issue 3.

Satprem, *Sri Aurobindo or the Adventure of Consciousness.*

Schafer R. Murray, *The Tuning of the World.*

Schweitzer Glenn, *Rewiring Tinnitus: How I Finally Found Relief From the Ringing in My Ears.*

BIBLIOGRAPHY

Steiner Rudolf, *The Education of the Child in the Light of Anthroposophy.*

Stevens Christine, *The Healing Power of Rhythm: A Handbook for Mind-Body Medicine.*

Thaut Michael H. & Hodges Donald A. (ed.), *The Oxford Handbook of Music and the Brain.*

Tolle Eckhart, *The Power Of Now* en *A New Earth.*

Upledger John E., *Craniosacral Therapy.*

Valone Thomas, *Zero Point Energy: The Fuel of the Future.*

von Helmholtz Hermann, *Über die Erhaltung der Kraft.*

Wheeler Barbara L. (ed.), *Music Therapy Handbook.*

A WORD OF THANKS

I would like to express my sincere gratitude to everyone who contributed to the realization of this book: Marie-Agnès Servais, Marc De Neve, Naofumi Yazaki, Heidi Coenen, Caroline Kromwel, Johan Rosvelds, Jonas Slaats, and Kim Ibens. Your support and expertise were invaluable throughout this project. Thank you for your valuable collaboration and dedication.

Healing Symphony
My Discovery of Healing in the Silence of Music

Didier François

Version 1.0

*

Yunus Publishing
Bolderberg, 2024

*

ISBN print: 9789492689344
D/2024/12.808/4

ISBN ebook: 9789492689351

*

Cover photograph:
Alex Piltz

*